The Greening of the Willow Bough

A Book of Poetry

by Sharlyn Guthrie

Copyright © 2019 by Sharlyn Guthrie. All rights reserved.

No portion of this book may be reproduced, stored in a retrieval system, or transmitted in any form or by any means without prior written permission of the publisher. Requests for permission or information should be submitted via email to sharlyngg@yahoo.com

ISBN-9781090405777

Table of Contents

PREFACE 1
WORSHIP 5
    PURPOSED FOR PRAISE 7
    CREATION'S SONG 8
    AWAKEN MY SENSES 10
    PRECIOUS HOLY SPIRIT 11
    GOD IS GREAT 12
    GOD OF NO NEED 13
    O COME LET US ADORE HIM 14
    THE WORD 16
    FOR WHO YOU ARE 17
    MY ALL IN ALL 18
GRACE UPON GRACE 19
    ONE TINY TENDER SHOOT 21
    COME GUILTY LEAVE FREE 22
    WHO I AM 23
    THE BAPTISM AT LESTER RICHEY'S FARM 24
    REGRETFUL WORDS 26
    QUIET TIME 27
    BREATHE 28
    CONDEMNED 30
    WELCOME HOME 31
    BOLD DICHOTOMY 32
    NAOMI PONDERS 33
    A SHEEP'S TALE 34
STRUGGLES 35
    A PATH UNKNOWN 37
    FEELING AGAIN 38
    THE FRAGILE BOWL 39
    COFFEE SHOP CATHARSIS 40
    WHAT OF THIS CROSS 42
    THE PROBLEM WITH DYING TO SELF 43

UNWELCOME GUEST	44
SEQUENCE OF JOY	45
IRON CLAD TRUTH	46
ON SILVER WINGS	47
THIRSTY	48
MINDSET MATTERS	49
IMPATIENCE KNOCKS	50
FAITH SENSED	52
GROWING COLD	53
INSIDIOUS INFESTATION	54
FORGIVE US	55
THE SEND-OFF	56
SEEING JESUS; BEING JESUS	**59**
THE BEGGAR OF PLAYA ICACOS	61
I SEE CHILDREN	62
UGANDA, MY LOVELY	63
THE BABY I CAN'T FORGET	64
HELPLESSNESS	65
CULTURE SHOCK	66
YEARNING TO RETURN	67
STREET PRAYERS	68
IRON CLAD TRUTH	69
FAMILY REDEFINED	70
TAG! YOU'RE WHO?	72
BLOSSOM	73
A PRAYER AND A PROMISE	74
SINCE I SAW YOU LAST	75
A PRAYER IN THE WITCHING HOUR	76
DISGUISED	78
LOVE AND ROMANCE	**79**
I BELIEVE YOU STILL	81
ALL SHOOK UP AT THE HOP	82
TRUE LOVE, YOU AND ME LOVE	85
UNITY	86

YOUR HANDS SPEAK LOVE	87
ONE MOMENT	88
DAILY HABIT	89
MY DAY FRIDAY	90
MORE THAN A VALENTINE	91
FOR THE LOVE OF COFFEE	92
70 YEAR PORTRAIT OF A MAARRIAGE	94
LOVE BY COMPARISON	95
FAMILY	97
WISH UPON A WILLOW	99
HOUSE RULES	100
FIRSTBORN	101
MASTER OF THE MIDDLE	102
DIMPLED DAYDREAMER	103
TO YOU, MY DAUGHTERS IN LAW AND LOVE	104
SWEET BABY	105
A METAMORPHOSIS	106
TREMORS	107
ALL THIS AND MORE	108
MIXTURE OF SWEETNESS	109
I AM ME	110
HOPE	111
A GIFT THAT KEEPS ON GIVING	112
OUR BROWN EYED GIRL	113
SOMETHING ABOUT THIS BOY	114
ENDOWED MEMORY	115
GARDEN SECRET	116
VIOLETS ON HER WINDOWSILL	118
MAMA'S SEWING MACHINE	120
GEODES	123
A SIMPLY WONDERFUL CHRISTMAS	124
THE WANDERLUST	125
DOORS	126
I AM FROM CALICO	128

EVERYONE NEEDS AN UNCLE JERRY	129
IT MIGHT BE A STRETCH	130
CAN YOU HEAR ME NOW?	132
THE LAST TO LEAVE	133
TIMES AND SEASONS	**135**
ELEMENTAL ARTISTRY	137
WILLOW SONGS	138
THREE ROBUST ROBINS	139
CONTEMPLATING SPRING	140
HAIL	141
SUMMER'S FIRST ROSE	142
CLOTHESLINE CLEAN	143
GARDEN ENCOUNTERS	144
SCHOOL DAYS	146
ODE TO FALL	147
FOREVER FALL	148
NOW IT'S NOVEMBER	149
DECEMBER DELIGHTS	150
EVERGREEN: ISAIAH 53	151
FOR JUST ONE DAY	152
LIGHTS OF CHRISTMAS	154
COMFORT AND JOY	155
TWO YEARS CONVERGED	156
NEW YEAR'S EVE	157
BACK TO THE FUTURE	158
UNINVITED	159
PERSPECTIVE	160
FOR THE YOUNG	**161**
SWISH, HUSH, SHUSH-A-BYE	163
OF WINGS AND THINGS	164
UMBRELLAS	165
THE TALE OF HALEY HALL	166
HOLD THAT PENCIL	168
CHILLS	169

ARRIVAL AND SURVIVAL OF THE CITY KIDS 170

A BUNNY AND PIG TALE 172

COOKIES 173

HIDE AND SQUEAK 174

LOOSE LIPS SINK SHIPS 175

ANGER'S PATH 176

LEGEND OF A BUSH AND A TREE..177

A LITTLE MORE 178

WHIMSY 179

BEGINNER'S ANGST 181

YOUR SMILE 182

TO ASK OR NOT TO ASK 183

HOW I GET AROUND 184

RUMMAGING AND REMINISCING 185

SO I'VE BEEN THINKING...186

REVELATION 187

THE PROBLEM WITH STARTING A DIET 188

TO DO OR NOT TO DO..189

SELF MOTIVATION 190

THE LAST DONUT 191

SHOPPING EXPERT, FABULOUS FRIEND 192

JADED 194

I MIGHT BE CRAZY 195

FOOLS 196

A VISITOR'S CANADIAN ANTHEM..197

FISHIN' FOR MEN 198

TOO MUCH INFORMATION 201

RESOLVE 202

THE STRAY 203

THREE HAIKUS 204

COMPLEX 205

MECHANICAL 206

NUMBER CRUNCHING 207

I WOULD IF I COULD 208

LESSON IN HUMILITY	209
SOMETHING	210
HOW TO MEASURE THE IMMEASUREABLE	211
PLAY TIME	212
GUILTY	213
POETIC INJUSTICE	214
WORD ART	215
WONDER	**217**
DREAMS AND THINGS	219
I LOVE	220
TEAL	221
HOPE EMERGES	222
THE REASON FOR A FLOWER	223
CLOTHESLINE CLEAN	224
IMPOSSIBLE THINGS	225
MAMA'S GIFT	226
OF HIM AND YOU	227
INCONGRUITY	228
REVERIE	229
OF SKY AND SEA	230
SWITCH OFF THE LAMP	231
JUST THE BASICS	232
LASTS AND FIRSTS	233

PREFACE

I have always enjoyed writing, although I abandoned the practice during the parenting small children phase of life. Then I met someone who introduced herself as a writer, and as I began telling her that I enjoy writing as well, she silenced me with this, "There is only one difference between a writer and one who enjoys writing. A writer is one who writes." That, and some personal crises encountered around the same time, moved me from *one who enjoys writing* to *one who writes*.

This book of poetry is my first published literary work, which I have been told is not the recommended course for a "serious author" to take. But a conformist I am not, so I will take my chances. Poetry is my passion, and each poem a tiny keyhole through which one may peek into my soul and ultimately, I hope, into the heart and character of God, to whom I have dedicated my life. Sometimes I write to clarify my own thinking; sometimes to share insights; other times to inspire or entertain. Throughout the book I have identified several poetic forms. I did this for two reasons: so that you can research these forms for yourself if you wish, and so you won't be concerned that I've lost my mind when you encounter them! I enjoy the challenge of trying out various poetic styles, as well as the freedom to invent my own.

Perhaps teaching the alphabet and early reading to preschoolers and kindergartners over the past 40+ years has played a part in my view of poetry as word play— an exercise in selecting words that entertain, inform, challenge; words that fit each chosen rhyme and rhythm scheme; words that make a visually and/or phonetically meaningful statement. Sometimes I choose to use standard rules of punctuation; other times the absence of punctuation makes a statement of its own. So, before you assume the worst, please consider why I may have included or omitted certain elements that are common in prose.

My title, "The Greening of the Willow Bough," is taken from a line of a poem contained within these pages. Maybe this knowledge (if nothing else) will keep you reading until you find it. I chose the title because it, as well as the poem from which it is taken, encompasses so many of the themes of my poetry...life, grace, growth, seasons, roots, family, and even my return to writing. The poem was inspired by a picture I took from my deck in Iowa one spring, but the picture wasn't clear enough or inspiring enough to use as my cover, so I commissioned Aubree (Meeker) Pinckney, a former student and talented artist, to paint a suitable cover. She met and exceeded all my expectations, and the painting now graces my wall, inspiring me daily. You can find and follow Aubree's work here:
https://www.facebook.com/TickledPinckneyDesigns/

(continued)

You will find my poems arranged in sections—sections that make sense to me according to how various aspects of my life are prioritized. Worship is the basis for everything I am; everything I think; everything I do. It is also how I begin each day, so in my mind it had to be first. Although the remaining sections are eclectic, common threads run throughout, as I cannot conceive a world void of beauty and grace; or void of the God who makes both beauty and grace possible; or void of God's image clearly visible in each and every human being He has created. While some sections (especially the first few) may be thoughtful and serious, others are humorous, whimsical, and playful. If you find that you are attracted to a particular section or a particular style of poetry more than others, I celebrate those preferences with you.

All illustrations in the "For the Young" section were created by my amazing and well above average grandchildren: Noah, Claire, Selah, Josie, Hope, Olive, Abigail, and Simeon. Many poems contained within these pages were inspired by them, as well.

"I don't understand poetry," is an oft' repeated sentiment. This has only challenged me to write with such readers in mind. I strive to make my poems readable and relatable, including the poems that are personal in nature. I desire for my readers to be inspired— not only by spiritual themes, but by the care taken in crafting each poem and the collection as a whole. I truly hope that you find one or more of my offerings worth pondering, revisiting, committing to memory, or sharing.

I am truly humbled that you are setting out to read this work of my heart and hands. If you find it noteworthy, I would appreciate you letting me know, and I also hope you will recommend it to others; a Kindle review would be awesome! Sharing individual poems of mine in a classroom or group setting is not only acceptable, it is a high compliment; but please be sure to identify me as the author. And if you wish to reprint a poem I authored, kindly request my permission first.

WORSHIP

Worship elevates the One who is above all

to his rightful place.

Here I humbly offer my words as worship

to He who alone is worthy

Worship the Lord in the splendor of holiness

Psalm 96: 9a

PURPOSED FOR PRAISE

I was created to praise you;
Charged upon heeding your call
To sing and desire to lift up
Your holy name higher than all.

All of your handiwork beckons,
Attracting my eyes to your grace;
Worthy are you beyond any on earth;
I yearn for a glimpse of your face.

I would be miserably selfish,
Lost and depressed without you.
Praise takes me higher and higher
Enlarging my heart with my view.

I was created to praise you;
Bring glory to your holy name
Speak of your wisdom, delight in your love,
Forever your goodness proclaim

CREATION'S SONG

Oh mystical, musical Presence
without beginning or end;
voice of three, yet One in its essence:
a lilting tenor of wind
over bass booming thunderous and wild
by pure tones of the Word reconciled.

Oh Voice shaking all the foundations
of what was yet to be made
in harmonious, pure undulations
as base and ballast were laid.
Great I AM moves with tremulous sweep
chanting, "Let there be..." into the deep.

*Holy, Holy, Holy is the Lord God, Almighty,
Who was and Who is and Who is to come!*

Oh Composer of body and spirit
forged in the image of God,
so to honor God's Word and to fear it
while ruling the beasts and sod,
orchestrating their care and provision
in sync with the Master Musician.

Oh Creator of holy acclaim
Who over creation stood
poised to view Your work and proclaim,
"Behold, it is very good!"
then led morning stars in their singing
with shouts of glad angel choirs ringing.

*Holy, Holy, Holy is the Lord God, Almighty,
Who was and Who is and Who is to come!*

Oh high, humorous Virtuoso,
maker of rhythm and rhyme,
Who transcribes creature noises in scherzo,
varied in tempo and time;
then in cycles of life stays their course
by intrinsic, intuitive force.

(continued)

Oh immanent, sovereign Conductor,
arranger of varied parts,
blending anthems and hymns in nature
to the trill of lovers' hearts.
Trees clap softly to meadowlark's song
as a cadence of crickets plays on.

Holy, Holy, Holy is the Lord God, Almighty,
Who was and Who is and Who is to come!

Oh Maestro of mercy and justice,
the sweetest duet by far—
born of flesh, yet holy and blameless,
now branded with Satan's scar.
Yet the dirge became jubilation;
You arose, and proclaimed vindication.

Oh infinite, timeless Transposer
tuning each age to Your grace,
preparing to slay the imposer
and then to reveal Your face
when our crowns at Your feet have been laid
and the great final movement is played.

Holy, Holy, Holy is the Lord God, Almighty,
Who was and Who is and Who is to come!

(Refrain is from Revelation 4:8 New American Standard Version Bible)

AWAKEN MY SENSES

Your fragrance is the very air
I breathe, O my God,
Emanating from Your being
An aroma sweet and pure
Like baking bread,
Aloe, lilacs, lavender, and myrrh;
O my God, let Your sweet aroma fill me.

Your beauty is delightfully
Revealed, O my God,
Radiating from Your presence
An awesome, glorious sight
Like rare gemstones,
Rainbows, fire, angel wings, and light;
O my God, let Your lovely vision thrill me.

Your melody is soothing
To my ears, O my God,
Sung in quiet strains accompanied
By the music of the earth
Like gurgling brooks,
Locust, bullfrogs, ocean waves, and mirth;
O my God, let Your comforting voice still me.

Your taste is sweeter to my mouth
Than wine, O my God,
Springing from an endless fountain
So my hungry soul is fed
With milk and honey, manna, water,
Vegetables, and bread;
O my God, let Your living food instill me.

Your touch incites a longing
In my breast, O my God,
Everlasting arms enfold me;
They're my solace and my peace
Like sand and sun, babies, blankets,
Rose petals, and fleece;
O my God, let Your loving touch fulfill me.

PRECIOUS HOLY SPIRIT

precious Holy Spirit
dwelling deep inside my soul
cheering with Your presence
making the broken whole
whispering words of comfort
breathing through my fear
holding me in silence
wiping every tear
endowing with Your wisdom
emboldening with power
surprising with Your wonders
every waking hour
strengthening arms for labor
and legs to run each race
filling days with praise
and nights with amazing grace
counseling in my confusion
guiding through the unknown
allowing peace to enfold me
making this body Your home

GOD IS GREAT

God is great!
...Great in power.
Mountains tremble, oceans roar!
Life lavished on
Creature, flower
Multiplies from shore to shore.

God is great!
...Great in beauty.
At His sight creation sings!
Rainbow fire
All-consuming,
Graced with jewels and angel wings.

God is great!
...Great in knowledge.
Knows my longings and my frame!
Richest depths of
Unsearched wisdom
Calls each child and star by name.

God is great!
...Great in justice.
Holy standard of the law!
Righteous Judge
Who knows no equal,
Substitute for human flaw.

God is great!
...Great in mercy.
Oh, what suffering, pain, and grief
Raised this creature
Weak and lowly,
Brought my hungering soul relief!

God is great
Beyond all measure...
Sovereign, holy, faithful, good!
Heart of mine,
Behold your Treasure,
Known, yet never understood.

GOD OF NO NEED

God of Life who cannot be needy
Or helpless or tired or worn
Clothed fully in light and in beauty
Without garments or jewels to adorn;
Whose power and strength can't be measured
Or equaled in earth sky or sea;
God who moves and breathes unrestricted
By time space or boundary;
Who owns all the wealth of the nations
Granting gifts we can never repay;
Whose mercies are new every morning
Unfathomable in every way…
What scholar has been Your advisor?
What comfort have You ever sought?
When did you need a reminder
Of something You simply forgot?
How deep is Your wisdom and knowledge!
So deep it can never be known!
Yet it's here in this heart frail and broken
You desire to reign on Your throne.
I simply cannot understand it;
The knowledge for me is too high.
God has come to this place
With His love and His grace
As my soul cries out, "Who am I?"
Self-sufficient One, You incite me
To view with loathing my needs.
With one breath of grace
And a glimpse of Your face
In wonder I fall to my knees.

O COME LET US ADORE HIM

O
Wow!
How   fitting
How   appropriate
How perfectly delightful
What   a great privilege
What an   opportunity
How   marvelous
Awesome!
O

Come
Take a break.
Cease your labor.
Whatever it is, it can wait
Lay down your book, golf club, fishing pole
Dry your hands; tie your shoes; close the door
Drive the old beater that needs a new muffler
Ride your motorcycle. Drive your sports car
Strap the kids into the mini-van
    Take a bus   Hail a cab
   Ride a bicycle   Rollerblade
    Use a cane   or walker
     Just...   come

Let
Allow
Permit
Confess frailties
Open mind and heart
Disallow fear and doubt
Shun platitudes (praise god)
Adjust attitude (Praise God!)
Gently shush your fussing child
Ignore the peeling ceiling plaster
Shrug off the squawking sound system
Exchange self-consciousness for God-consciousness
Enable the Holy Spirit; acknowledge His presence; expect His response
Relinquish control
Prepare
Give in
Let

Us
You and I
The redeemed
The chosen ones
Simpletons
Nerds
Businessmen and battered wives
Politicians, prostitutes, police officers
Toddlers, teenagers
Adults, senior citizens
Construction workers,
Doctors, teachers, soldiers
Wealthy, wicked, wounded
Athletes, alcoholics, addicts
Pursued by God, Bought with blood
Found, forgiven, freed
His body   The church
Fused   As one
We   Us

Adore
Exalt
Praise
Admire
Bow down
Make a joyful noise
Sing appealing songs with feeling
Voices blended, praise ascended
Regard with awe
Lift holy hands
Gaze upon
Celebrate
Magnify
Worship
Dance
Honor
Extol
Love
Adore

Him
God   Holy One   I Am
Jehovah   Creator   Yahweh
Wonderful Counselor, Lord God Almighty
The Alpha and Omega, Prince of Peace
Ruler of all things, Everlasting Father
King of Kings and Lord of Lords
Lion of Judah, The Word, Him

O Come, Let Us Adore Him!

THE WORD

The Word
Beginning breath
Planning, forming, speaking
I worship, awed by His power
Jesus

The earth
Empty, shapeless
Feeding, grounding, yielding,
I till, blessed in co-creating
Terrain

Mountain
Solid, stately
Rising, looming, guiding
I ascend, drunk on angel air
High peak

Forest
Deep, compelling
Growing, twining, thriving
I enter, drawn by His Presence
Woodland

Water
Cool refreshment
Trickling, rushing, flowing
I plunge, exhilarated, cleansed
River

The Sky
Endless azure
Dazzling, drizzling, stirring
I inhale, soul and lungs refreshed
Expanse

Jesus
Savior, Shepherd
Bleeding, dying, living
I trust, secure within His love
The Word

FOR WHO YOU ARE

You are truly a God of mercy and grace,
A Father who sees me in every dark place
And loves me no matter the deeds that I do,
The thoughts that I think, or the things I go through;

Your name is Almighty, Creator, Yahweh,
Yet You embrace me with Your arms every day.
I can't comprehend, Lord, why Your knees would bend
So low to the earth to make me Your friend.

But God, I am grateful. I can't say enough
Of blessings You've brought through the times that were tough.
I ask Your forgiveness for doubting Your care;
Each time I have stumbled You've always been there.

I can't earn your love, buy, or trade it –it's free!
Not one thing I do will change Your love for me.
So rather than ask for small favors today
I bask in Your presence and praise as I pray.

MY ALL IN ALL

God indivisible...
Perfect, Immutable,
Incomprehensible!
My All in All.

One in three, three in one
Unified Deity
Abba, Spirit, God's Son
My Hope, my Peace

Omniscient, holy, wise
Triune Identity
Word, Breath, and El Shaddai
My Truth, my Rock

Merciful, sovereign, just
All-present and in me
In you I wholly trust
My Bread, my Vine

God indivisible...
Perfect, Immutable,
Incomprehensible!
My All in All

GRACE UPON GRACE

I cannot tell you where Grace begins

or where it ends. But this I know:

From His hand I have received

grace upon grace

ONE TINY TENDER SHOOT

From barren soil, drought-stricken, parched
One tiny tender Shoot appeared.
So plain and homely was its form
It was not welcomed nor revered
Where men in sullen shadows marched.

Abundant sorrow shame and grief
Bent the Sprout low to the ground,
So smitten and afflicted here
That even God most surely frowned,
Making its earthly visit brief.

I saw through eyes blind and diseased;
I saw, and yet assumed the worst:
Death was the end –His just reward,
But of the dead He was the first
To end its curse, and God was pleased!

Abundant love coursed through His veins,
Abundant pardon, mercy, grace
Gushed from violent gaping wounds,
Compassion dripping from His face;
Only His righteousness remains.

Broken and bathed in Jesus' blood
My sins are gone, my sight restored!
The bud, once stricken, scorned, despised
Now lives; is treasured and adored;
Once-thirsty soil quenched by the flood.

Now life abundant, joy, and peace
Sustain my spirit, soul, and mind!
I feast on Him, my daily bread,
And drink His water, milk, and wine…
Abundant gifts that never cease!

(Based on Isaiah 53 and 55:1)

COME GUILTY LEAVE FREE

Come guilty one,
Look on the Guiltless.
Come to the cross;
He is calling to you.
Love drew you here,
Not condemnation.
Look at him now
Wounded and torn
Because of love...

Why would a king
Step down from Heaven;
Take on the weight
Of your guilt and mine?
Humble beyond
All comprehension;
Eager to serve;
Willing to die
Because of love...

Lay down your load;
No need to carry
Pain and regret
For your past crimes.
Jesus redeemed
Every transgression;
Traded his life
For yours and mine
Because of love...

WHO I AM

Give me a holy untainted self-view.
When I look in the mirror let me see only You;
Not who I was—sin-battered and sore—
My old self doesn't exist anymore.

Satan wants me to see myself wicked and lame.
He wants me to walk with my head hung in shame.
When I do that, I mock the great price that You paid.
You died for nothing if I wasn't re-made.

Your blood washed me clean, even whiter than snow.
My countenance should glisten, my spirit should glow.
So, help me remember with each day's new start
I'm precious to You and I have a good heart.

THE BAPTISM AT LESTER RICHEY'S FARM

Andy was a druggie in a gritty hard-rock band.
Carl was a warlock -yes, in Iowa's heartland.
Each of them found Jesus and vowed to take a stand.
They wanted to be baptized and follow Christ's command.

Sue's daddy was the mayor of our tiny little town.
Elena went to homecoming and came home with the crown.
They gave their lives to Jesus along with Molly Brown,
And they'll wade into the river to lay their egos down.

Corey went to school but he didn't really care.
Jimmy sat behind him and blew spitballs in his hair.
Kevin was so stoned he had an empty, haunting stare.
They all have been redeemed, so on Sunday, they'll be there.

At the farm of Lester Richey just past McGuire Bend,
Come down to the river. Bring your neighbors and your friends.
We'll be shouting, "Hallelujah!" and the joy will never end.
All these lives have been transformed, though it's hard to comprehend.

Oh, we gathered at the river on that thirteenth day of June.
We listened to some preaching 'til it was almost noon.
We sang "Amazing Grace" while Andy strummed the tune.
Twenty-six were baptized. It ended way too soon.

And as I watched, mesmerized on that farmer's sacred shore
God's Spirit seared the memory on my heart forevermore...

Waist-high in the water and ankle-deep in mud
They told how Jesus cleansed them with His life-giving blood;
And while the cow sat blinking and chewing on her cud
In Father, Son, and Spirit each was plunged beneath the flood,

Whenever folks are baptized, I drift back to that morn
Surrounded by the soybeans and endless rows of corn.
Many hearts to God were yielded; old allegiances were torn.
Each was raised to live in Christ as one who was reborn.

Now I've recited liturgies and prayed the hallowed prayer.
I've been to huge tent meetings out in the open air.
I've visited cathedrals, but nothing can compare
To that gathering by the river and the Spirit's presence there.

(continued)

At the farm of Lester Richey just past McGuire Bend,
we came down to the river, brought our neighbors and our friends.
We shouted, "Hallelujah!" and the joy will never end.
It was there that many died and were raised to life again.

NOTE: *The Baptism at Lester Richey's Farm* is based on an actual baptism that took place near Stratford, Iowa on June 13, 1971— one that I was privileged to attend. God moved mightily through Carl and Andy after bringing them both to salvation. The Bible studies they led drew hundreds of teenagers from several nearby communities.

Those of us who already knew Jesus experienced amazement, humility, and great joy as friends and classmates came to know Him, too. The baptism at Lester Richey's farm was only the first of several such baptisms.

Carl became a missionary. Andy is an elder of the church that began as a result of that summer's events. Lester Richey was the actual farmer who allowed use of his property. All other names in this story are fictional, although God continues to work in and through a number of individuals who came to faith and were baptized in the river near Stratford, Iowa in 1971.

REGRETFUL WORDS

Words of anger
Words of bile
Tumbled out
Into the pile
Of rubbish
Being slung
Without a thought.

But oh they stung
And what I ought
To have said
Instead
Plays on repeat
In my mind-
I can't rewind
And I'm the one
To blame.

No words
Can fully heal
Your wounds-
Even my mumbled
I'm sorry
Seemed lame;
But there
With hurt
Smeared on
Your face
Like so much mud...

You gave me grace.

QUIET TIME

I sit, Bible in hand, body erect.
I'm groggy, but the coffee's nearly brewed.
My time with God I try not to neglect,
although unbidden thoughts sometimes intrude."

This half an hour is His, and His alone.
I rise before my husband and the dawn
with no computer, music, or cell-phone.
Alas, five minutes is already gone.

"Lord, I invite You now into this day."
Fly, how dare you land upon my nose?
"Be my first thought as I walk in Your way."
Did I forget nail polish on my toes?

"Oh God, You are most worthy of my praise."
Perhaps I ought to use another name-
Almighty, Adonai, Ancient of Days...
I wonder if the Packers won their game.

"Lord, forgive my weak and wandering mind."
Is this the day I need to leave at eight?
"Into Your care my thoughts I now resign."
I'd better hurry so I won't be late.

"Guide and direct me, keep me free from sin."
Can't wait to share the juicy news I've got.
"Lord, please restore my focus once again."
I'd better go turn off the coffee pot.

"Oh yes, Father, and if it is Your will,"
This is my most repeated daily prayer.
"Help my students listen and be still."
They're all ADHD I do declare!

~~~

 "And I, unhappy one and poorest of men, how shall I bring you into my house, I who scarce know how to spend a half hour devoutly? And would that I spent once, even one half-hour worthily." -Thomas a Kempis *Imitations of Christ*

"...What, could ye not watch with me one hour?" –Jesus
(Matthew 26:40 King James Version Bible)

BREATHE

From the sea fate called to me,
harmless 'round my ankles danced.
Brimming with frivolity
my heart leaped in, taking the chance.

Like my mood the waves were grand,
spurting high above the swells,
blithely scooping up the sand,
rearranging all the shells.

Eagerly I caught the next,
rode its fluid, forceful back,
felt the muscle that it flexed-
surging strength my spirit lacked.

Repeatedly I safely lit
with abandon, bliss, and pride.
I rode each crest with half a wit
trusting fluctuating tide.

Heedless, forging deeper still,
I left the safety of the shore
seeking yet a greater thrill
above the ocean's mighty roar.

At last I rode so deep, so far
my feeble arms could never swim
to yonder shore or distant bar;
I journeyed there upon a whim.

Until then, fate was my friend.
Suddenly he turned about-
turned deserter in the end,
mimicking my panicked shout.

Breakers crashed above my head,
felled me with tremendous force.
I sank down with fear and dread,
gulped salt water and remorse.

Flailing arms grasped liquid air.
Vain, I'd failed to leash my board.
Absorbed with merriment, I'd dared
to take my eyes off of the Lord.

(continued)

Hopeless, helpless I was tossed.
Billows whirled and whipped about.
I knew then that all was lost;
perceived it well without a doubt.

As the ocean roiled and seethed
sturdy arms lifted my head
bidding me to simply breathe…
"Breathe!" is all the lifeguard said.

One breath, I think of it, amazed!
Strength restored, spirit renewed.
Refocusing my fickle gaze
I saw that I had been pursued.

Foolishly I'd rushed to play.
Wiser eyes followed me there.
Though I drifted far away
He marked my every move with care.

I soon inhaled with greater ease.
Deft, He steered me to the shore.
With gratitude my heart was seized.
The lifeguard gave me life once more.

CONDEMNED

The heart speaks

How could you be so ignorant, my friend,
When you agreed your graceless hand to lend?
Did you believe for once you might succeed;
Escape misfortune through a noble deed?

Now you have failed not only to impress,
But to avoid making a royal mess.
Not only did you let me play the fool,
But opened up this heart to ridicule.

Don't you recall the words you often heard?
Your father, teachers, and your friends concurred.
They said you never would amount to much;
Things seem to go to pieces with your touch.

You may as well go lick your wounds and weep,
Or throw yourself upon a garbage heap.
Preserve this in your memory and then
You won't risk trying anything again.

The Spirit speaks

O heart, be still and hear my whispering voice.
You're my delight; a child of mine by choice.
I saw your unformed substance and I knew
How best to mold you. Please believe it's true.

The error that you've made is very small;
Cleansed by my blood on Calvary once for all.
So, calm your anxious thoughts and right your wrongs.
I'll salve you with my presence and with songs.

I've heard the lies hurled at you, precious heart-
Lies striking you just like a flaming dart.
You listen, and yourself harshly condemn.
Who do you think is greater, I or them?

I came to heal you, heart, and bind your sores;
Abundant life I offer you, and more. Draw near with confidence; forget the past.
Let truth assure you that my love will last.

"It is by our actions that we know we are living in the truth, so we will be confident when we stand before the Lord, even if our hearts condemn us. For God is greater than our hearts, and he knows everything." (I John 3: 19-20 New Living Translation Bible)

WELCOME HOME

Warmth wrapped its long arms around me as I entered the cozy family room. It emanated from the handshakes and smiles that greeted me. It crackled inside the fireplace and flowed through me as I sipped hot chocolate and nibbled fresh-baked banana bread.

Curiosity pulled me into the conversation. It nudged with each introduction and needled through the small talk. It glimmered in the others' eyes. It licked my fingers and curled up on my lap -cautious, but willing to take a risk.

Variety caught me by surprise, binding me into the common cord that wound through the evening. It directed music, shaped prayer requests, and expounded on the Scriptures. It projected from eclectically decorated walls. It delineated opinions, personalities, and backgrounds, piquing my interest. And it cleverly defined our humble troupe.

Comfort crept in to replace caution, coaxing off protective layers and drawing my stocking feet up into the arm chair. It convinced me to relax and be myself —not perfect, just real. It eased strained features and curved set lips. It carried me into my Father's presence.

Renewal began, flickering with hope's tiniest ray, thawing the perimeter of a stone-cold heart. It bowed my head and brought me to my knees, weary and broken. It revealed my folly and my pride, evoking repentance. It was portrayed in the warmth and comfort of a home and in the imperfect, varied, and devoted members of Christ's body assembled there. Complete healing still seemed distant, but hope insured it would come.

BOLD DICHOTOMY
(an acrostic)

Blemished by men who abused her
Oppressed by the enemy's voice
Livid with rage and hounded by shame
Drusilla seduced men by choice

Brazen, she flaunted her figure
Obsessed with her cheap little tricks
Levied fierce wounds on her victims
Duping the simple for kicks

Beguiled, the naïve were attracted
Oblivious to her disease
Laughing, she led them to Hades
Defiling their honor with ease

But as her suitors paraded
One gazed right into her soul
Looked on her cold heart with pity
Damned her demons to Sheol

Blood was required for her purchase
Only His blood to be sure
Love paid the ultimate ransom
Declaring the prostitute pure

Broken, she fell down before Him
Owned the full guilt of her wrongs
Loudly proclaimed Him her Master
Danced and exulted with songs

Blushing duplicitous leaders
Opted to pelt her with clay
Loathed the barefaced interloper
Distastefully spoiling their day

Batter and bruise her, said Jesus.
Or have you once happened to sin?
Lob stones only if you are perfect.
Do step right on up and begin.

Beaten, each slowly retreated 'til
Only the woman remained
Lustrous in clean garments flowing
Devoid of each blemish and stain.

NAOMI PONDERS

Because of you, wee one, who coos in the crook of my withered arm; because of you I know my God remembers.

Hunger banished my family from our home. Refugees we were— beset by weariness, suppressed by loneliness in a strange, distant land. Discouragement and fear stalked us. Death overtook us. God dealt with me so bitterly I was certain I'd been forgotten. But all is well, wee one. Because of you I know my God remembers.

Because of you, precious one, who curls tiny fingers around my gnarled, arthritic one; because of you I know my God redeems.

What overwhelming loss I experienced! Your devoted grandfather and our two beloved sons were snatched from me. Who would comfort me? Who would further my family? Who even cared if I lived or died? Too old to marry, and too poor to support your mother, I begged her to leave me and return to her mother and father. She refused, fierce in her loyalty to me. Although I had nothing to offer her, she left the country of her birth. She was better to me than seven sons. Her humble, honorable actions caught your papa's eye. Your papa, my husband's kinsman, took pity on us. He has become our deliverer; our rescuer. I know my God redeems.

Because of you, little one, whose breath is warm and sweet against my wrinkled cheek; because of you I know my God rewards.

Hope had dispersed like chaff in the wind. Dreams had dissolved into tears. The outlook was dismal, bleak. This day, this moment, this fulfillment of hopes and dreams I dared not believe in or even wish for. But God smiled on me; smiled upon your mother; blessed His humble servants. Because of you I know my God rewards.

Because of you, cherished one, whose curious eyes quicken my aged heart and lighten my faltering steps. Because of you I know my God restores.

My home, my family, my lineage will endure. I am called blessed among Bethlehem's women. If my sons, Mahlon and Chilion, had lived and fathered many children, none would hold as much promise as you -my delightful grandson, Obed. You are my fulfillment, my future, my renewer of hopes and dreams. My nights are restful, my days filled with purpose. Because of you I know my God restores.

(a prose poem based on the book of Ruth)

A SHEEP'S TALE

I often wandered willfully too near the rocky edge.
That's how I lost my footing and landed on the ledge
Entangled in the briars, held fast by doubt and fear.
The Shepherd called with ardor. I pretended not to hear.

The enemy approached me dressed boldly in sheep clothes.
I smelled his acrid odor and glimpsed his pointed nose.
His raspy voice implored me to view the grassy glen
Where lively lambs romped blithely outside his wild wolf den.

The slopes were too confining. I yearned to kick my heels.
I ventured to the valley to learn how freedom feels.
I went just for a visit. I never planned to stay.
The enemy enticed me with his lies along the way.

The Shepherd kept on calling and I started to look up,
But the enemy entreated me to drink from pleasure's cup.
The last of my resistance dissolved before my eyes.
Pleasure dulled my senses, silencing the Shepherd's cries.

The valley was more dismal than it seemed from up above.
I missed the Shepherd's surety and his tender words of love.
But how could I return to Him? The climb was rough and steep,
And I'd surely face the judgment of the other mountain sheep.

Then I fell into a pit and sunk deep into the slime.
The walls were high, and wet, and slick ...too difficult to climb.
Others sneered and scoffed at me. My wool was foul and torn.
Nights were filled with terror, and days with cruel scorn.

There my shepherd found me in that lonely, shameful place.
He reached down through the muck, drew me into his embrace.
At the stream he healed my spirit, then washed me clean and pure.
On the rock-hard path of righteousness, he set my feet, secure.

My rescue cost a hefty price I found out, to my shame.
The wounds my shepherd suffered left deep scars that bore my name.
Still, he held a celebration when at last I reached the fold.
He will do the same for you. That is why this tale was told.

"He lifted me out of the slimy pit, out of the mud and mire;
He set my feet on a rock and gave me a firm place to stand."
(Psalm 40:2 New International Version Bible) Struggles

STRUGGLES

To trouble I am not immune;

It finds me as it finds you.

But struggles compel me to trust;

So, embrace them I must.

Consider it pure joy...whenever you face trials...because you know that the testing of your faith produces perseverance. James 1: 2-3

A PATH UNKNOWN

Today I walk along a path unknown;
I must admit I never would have come here on my own.
In fact, I don't know how I happened here,
Or where this path will lead; there is so much that is unclear.

But He knows when I sit and when I rise.
He hems me in before and then He hems me in behind.
And when I cry out in the dead of night
The darkness is not dark to Him; He fills it with His light.

Today it seems I have a choice to make.
I could denounce this path as some immense divine mistake,
Or I could view it as a chance to rest
Within my Father's loving arms, held safe against His breast.

For He knows when I sit and when I rise.
He hems me in before and then He hems me in behind.
And when I cry out in the dead of night
The darkness isn't dark to Him; He fills it with His light.

I don't know where or when this path will end.
But God, the mighty warrior, walks beside me as a friend.
His perfect love my anxious heart will still,
And over me He will rejoice, with songs my senses fill.

For He knows when I sit and when I rise.
He hems me in before and then He hems me in behind.
And when I cry out in the dead of night
The darkness isn't dark to Him; He fills it with His light.

Lord, you know when I sit and when I rise.
You hem me in before and then You hem me in behind.
And when I cry out in the dead of night
The darkness is not dark to You; You fill it with Your light.

(See Psalm 139 and Zephaniah 3:17)

FEELING AGAIN

I know how it feels not to feel a thing.
I'm hollow inside and it's hard to sing.
Nothing moves or evokes a tear.
Laughter is shallow and fails to cheer.
Events don't delight, impress, or excite.
Night turns to day and day to night.
Predictable, routine, and so mundane...
Thoughts, words and feelings seem inane.

I know how it feels to feel again;
Feelings flow freely from heart to pen.
Sorrow, exuberance-- both are embraced,
Filling the space that not-feeling erased.
Appreciation of detail abounds:
Intricate textures and complex sounds.
Melodies dance inside my soul
And blend with the senses to make me whole.

I wish I could tell you where to start
To renew the passions that once thrilled your heart.
It seems trite to tell you not to despair
And to keep your faith in the God who cares.
Yet He is the author of hope for each day
Wonderful Counselor, Truth, Light, and Way.
So trust, seek, and desire the Lord
And one day your joy will be restored.

THE FRAGILE BOWL

Life is great, the day is bright, I'm feeling satisfied.
It often seems that's just the time my faith is sorely tried.
I'll stretch a little higher, maybe now I'll reach my goal.
My fingertips have brushed, and now dislodged the fragile bowl.
In an instant confidence comes crashing at my feet.
There it lies in shattered slivers, threatening my defeat.
One moment all I strove for was nearly in my grasp.
In haste it was destroyed before the next moment elapsed.

This scene has been replayed, and now I ache with a desire
To sweep the pieces up and drop them in God's blazing fire.
His skillful hands mold broken shards into a vessel healed,
Each more exquisite than the last, His workmanship revealed.
The fire is hot, the process sometimes painful and severe;
But with each trial I'm learning better how to persevere.
When at last my vessel glistens, completed by His grace
I want to see more clearly the image of His face.

Exulting in my circumstance so tragic, yet assured
I find in Him the strength I need to patiently endure.
The confidence restored is in my Savior, not myself.
Tenderly I place it on a not-so-distant shelf.
Resplendent in its beauty, when I look at it, I see
A reflection of my Master where my handprints used to be.
New hope expands within me, stirred by the Spirit's breath;
A hope that never disappoints, and fears not even death.

(Based on Romans 5:3-5)

COFFEE SHOP CATHARSIS

We all know one another,
Or claim to be good friends,
Though it's rare to speak beyond our pleasantries.
We have our obligations
And urgent expectations;
Commitments to our precious families.

Our kinship draws us here,
Or perhaps a longing does;
A desire to see behind facades we're wearing.
So, on this afternoon
On the twenty-sixth of June
We risk our very selves with honest sharing.

We've claimed a private corner,
Or at least a distant one.
We're undisturbed by others that surround us.
How many times this year
Have I failed to see your tears?
I must admit that to your pain I was oblivious.

How can I claim to know you,
Or even claim to care?
The question stirs a haunting deep inside.
God met your deepest need;
Yet inwardly I grieve,
Wondering how I might have helped if I'd but tried.

And soon, before I know it,
Or take the time to think,
My own fickle façade has crumbled, too.
My frailties have been told,
At the risk of seeming bold.
Perhaps sharing my flaws will strengthen you.

Someone suggests we hold hands
And bow our heads to pray.
Into His mighty hands our cares are laid.
We came simply as friends;
We're sisters in the end,
When the roll and coffee bill is finally paid.

(continued)

Returning to our duties
Or to our separate homes,
Our bonds are stronger than they were before.
The fellowship was sweet
And honest and complete.
There's a fullness in our hearts we can't ignore.

WHAT OF THIS CROSS

What of this cross that lies across my way
Imploring that myself I should betray?
It reeks of putrid death; foreshadows pain.
Is that my name engraved across its grain?

What of this cross? I find it interferes
With plans, belongings, all that I hold dear.
Must every precious treasure be laid down?
Is there indeed no other way around?

What of this cross that emulates my Lord's,
Yet sparks among my loved ones such discord?
Fighting, dissension, arguments, and hate—
This cross does not bring peace, but separates.

What of this cross that makes my footsteps halt?
I must decide to die or to default.
Every allegiance I must now disown;
Take up this cross and carry it alone.

This cross I'll bear and boast of only He
Who leads the way and spilled His blood for me.
I shall not hesitate nor breathe a sigh;
But gain my life when self commits to die.

THE PROBLEM WITH DYING TO SELF

The problem with dying to self
Is that I'm so alive:
Opinions, dreams, desires…
What do I do with those? Kill them, too?
What would I have left then? Only You!
Once pride is buried with all that stuff
Would You really be enough?

The problem with dying to self
Is that it hurts too much:
Letting go, separation –loss.
You give new life they say. What kind?
Having once died, what pleasures will I find?
If aspirations all are lost
Will the pain be worth the cost?

Jesus, make these fears abate
And lead me on the painful path
That always leads to peace and you
Whether the route is rough or smooth;
Curved or straight; muddy or dry I won't deny
That you're the Master of my fate;
Death, end this vain debate.

UNWELCOME GUEST

From where you came
I do not know,
Nor do I know how you arrived.
I want to send you back
But you won't go—
Or stay where
I have tried to hide you.

You've come to take,
Take what you can;
For you have nothing good to give.
You want my joy; my sorrow
I would cede.
However,
It won't go without you.

If you could drown,
My tears would rise
Above your wanton, hungry eyes
And that would be your death.
But tears are
salve, not weapons.
They could never kill you.

So I will stare
You down until
You've taken all you came to steal,
While peace and joy remain
Abiding
To the end.
At last they'll overcome you.

SEQUENCE OF JOY

Like unexpected cool, refreshing rain
Showered on the evil and the just,
Joy seeps through lingering clouds of grief and pain,
Sprinkling those who do and do not trust.

On chance and circumstance this joy depends
...perilously totters on a rail.
A sudden gust or shifting of the winds
Topples and defeats its effort frail.

This joy erupts, but soon it must elapse,
As surely as a wilting withering leaf.
Beholden, it drifts just beyond my grasp,
A temporary bliss however brief.

Yet there exists a rare, uncommon joy
For those who lean upon the Father's breast;
One that doom and crisis can't destroy,
Regardless how they put it to the test.

Planted deep, this joy springs from the Source.
The Spirit tends His flourishing fruit with care.
Inspiring and efficacious force,
His bounteous, blessed gift He's pleased to share.

Still, joy is tempered here by sin and woe.
The bridegroom yearns to make my joy complete!
Consummate, boundless streams of joy will flow,
Immersing me before His mercy sea

IRON CLAD TRUTH

We humans are plentiful
And common as a populace.
Though we have many
Desirable qualities
Strength isn't our greatest asset;
But being connected –
In community, in relationship –
Strengthens us like nothing else.
Weakness make us vulnerable,
But hardship begets resilience.
Feet to the fire
We become pliable;
It is there, at our most vulnerable
That those who have been similarly
Challenged shape and
Encourage us to be everything
Our Master Craftsman intended.
Iron sharpens Iron;
One person sharpens another.

(Based on Proverbs 27:17)

ON SILVER WINGS
(a sestain)

Up, up on silver wings that kissed the sky
I rose, along with all my earthly fears.
Transported to vast, peaceful, sandy shores,
I entered through two wide and welcoming doors;
Then laughed, releasing thankful, joyful tears
To find the place I'd dreamed and dared to fly.

The place itself could make my spirit soar;
Then came another set of silver wings
Delivering flesh of my very flesh.
With gratefulness my heart rejoiced afresh,
Spilling over with a thousand things.
I felt that it could not contain one more.

Then broke the dawn —-a grinning, gleaming sun
Performing, skipping all along the waves;
Revealing diamonds mixed with grains of sand;
Embracing us with warm, far-reaching hand.
Worry, fear, that oft' my heart enslaved
Had vanished long before that day was done.

Along the sea I strolled beside my love,
Hand in hand, bare toes within its reach.
We traded thoughts and memories; hoped and dreamed
Of things impossible, or so it seemed.
Launching a kite, we ran along the beach
Watching our apprehensions sail above.

That bright and glorious day turned into days
Until our precious minutes all were spent.
The homeward journey I could not refuse
And yet I would if it were mine to choose.
Up, up again on silver wings I went
Above bronze clouds and evening's waning rays.

Love's gaze followed the progress of my flight
Making the journey harder yet to bear.
But soon anticipation conquered dread
As I envisioned what now lay ahead.
My welcome home would be so grand, so fair
I'd soon forget the sorrows of that night.

THIRSTY

I come with broken heart and wounded soul
Longing, seeking, thirsting for my God.
Like a deer I pant and crave the water
Trickling, running, gushing toward its goal.

I now boldly approach the river's shore.
I'll leap, immerse myself completely in it.
But at the water's edge I'm told I mustn't.
I may have only a drop and nothing more.

Before I drink I need to understand,
Study, memorize, gain knowledge of
Some basic truths about this precious water
And how and when it came to drench this land.

I'm thirsty, but someday I'll get to drink
So I learn of elements, amoeba, germs,
History, chemistry, philosophy…
My throat's so parched, that I can hardly think.

I'm smarter, but somehow I've lost my thirst.
Drinking is much harder than I guessed.
Now I know the dangers of just drinking
Without completely knowing water first.

My brother found a stream where he is urged
To jump right in just as he is, unlearned.
He's joyful, satisfied, and so refreshed,
But not half as smart as I, once he's emerged.

MINDSET MATTERS

Woe is me
Taxes are late
Moved up a bracket.
Sold stock to pay
Kids make a racket
A lot on my plate
Woe is me

How blessed I am
My miracle child
Means medical bills
And still I am thankful
I've got her pills
My worries are mild
How blessed I am

IMPATIENCE KNOCKS

Impatience knocks
begs me to play
throws discontent at me all day
makes me annoyed
with plans and rules
wisdom blocks

Impatience stays
gaining new ground
momentum gained, she sticks around
tossing her curves
and growing strong
life delays

Impatience goes
where're I go
follows behind a step or so
nudges me, nags
nips at my heels
never slows

Impatience sighs
shouts in my ear
"Hurry! move on! Don't linger here!"
breathes down my neck
clears her throat
peace denies

Impatience pokes
she agitates
like fingernail on a chalkboard grates
raises blood pressure
quickens pulse
pain provokes

Impatience raps
on tabletop
counts the seconds; tick…tick…tock
churns my stomach
makes me ill
vigor zaps

(continued)

Impatience frets
when I am tired
changes to frenzy when I'm ired
needles by day
disturbs by night
fuels regrets

Impatience steals
much of my day
moments of joy wishes away
dispels delight
With anger seethes
love conceals

Impatience flees
from Spirit's breath
knows her end; finds her death
gives way to peace
grows calm and still
Jesus sees

FAITH SENSED

Faith smells scent of rose
In February's snow
Sees a Picasso
In scribbles on the wall

Faith tastes sweet honey
Even as the bee stings
Hears true harmony
Within the battle call

Faith knows this moment
Exists beyond today
Feels the Father's heart
Beating steady through it all.

GROWING COLD

Cold! The body's growing cold
Inside alabaster walls
Insulated from the world,
Her house filled up with treasure.
Fingers 'round fine gems are curled.
Silence rings in hallowed halls
Haunted by the saints of old.

Cold! The body's growing cold,
Intent upon her purpose.
Self-protection was her choice.
Shoulder of indifference raised,
She ignored the Master's voice
In manner cool and callous.
Pride crept in, taking its hold.

Cold! The body's growing cold;
Stripped of her former glory
She lies wrapped in filmy gown,
Enticing other lovers.
Turning, she despised her crown—
Exchanged her wondrous story
For a tale easier told.

Once a holy fire burned
Deep within her pulsing breast;
Caused enlightened eyes to see
The world as Jesus saw it.
Charged with ardent urgency
She embraced the weak, oppressed;
Fanned the Flame for which they yearned.

Burn again, oh fire, burn!
Blaze within her fainting heart!
Melt the scales that blind her eyes,
And her nakedness expose.
Rouse her quick, before she dies!
Once again, your zeal impart.
Oh, first Love, to her return.

INSIDIOUS INFESTATION

Lord, have mercy on our nation
Fraught with evil infestation;
Evil from within, without
Fed with atheistic doubt.
Patriot's Day random explosions
Maim and kill, heightening emotions.
Boston's cries sound loud and clear
Across the airways far and near.

While cries of infants shriek above
The city of brotherly love
Unheeded, feign reported lest
Awareness stirs a hornets' nest.
Both acts are those of terrorists
Within our land so richly blessed,
Yet wayward, arrogant, Godless-
Lord, pray, how have we come to this?

FORGIVE US
(a sonnet)

Forgive us, precious Father, for we've strayed,
We sheep whose wretched lives you died to save.
in our haste to right our nation's wrongs,
Took up a battle that to you belongs.

We've chosen as our savior one whose deeds
Are fueled by lust for power and by greed—
A man who hides behind a thin disguise
Fueling his pride and boastfulness with lies.

The poor and weak by him are mocked and scorned;
Of men like this Your Word has often warned.
But we've invested so much in this fight
We now defend our misjudgments as right.

Humble us now, and in these crucial hours
Make Yourself known, make Your desires ours

THE SEND-OFF

The request came
To help make room
For a bed.
The dreaded bed –
The one hoped, prayed,
And fiercely fought against.
We had helped with other tasks—
Small ones. Easy ones.
This task was hard –
Epic for a man who had filled
Every minute with life
Even in the months before his death.
One glimpse of our friend
Told us it would be our last,
But of course, we didn't say so…
The love of his life knew too,
But saying it aloud might make it true,
So, we all carried on as usual
Even though there was
Nothing usual about this
Or him –
Pale as the sheets spread
Over his almost unrecognizable frame.
This man was deeply loved by the three of us
Standing there wishing we were gathered
To eat ice cream and play Dictionary;
Wishing we could all look away
So as not to see the inevitable.
He always joked, put us at ease,
Made us forget what he was facing.
But this day his eyes said
What his lips denied—
Pain replacing the twinkle; his body
Restless, ready to
Move on, completely spent
By the effort required
To get into bed.
Ragged, uneven breaths belied
The smile attempting to form
On his lips.

(continued)

We prayed for him, our hands holding his.
Prayed for mercy, strength, peace...
Things only possible
Through Jesus Christ whose grace
Made us not only friends
But siblings.
And he, with feeble voice
But valiant spirit
Promised to pray for us!
Our bags were packed for the
Long journey we embarked on the next day.
Sometime while
Crossing oceans and continents
To begin our Africa mission
Steve completed his earthly one
Arriving in Heaven,
The home for which he was created.
I have often imagined him
Marching right up to the throne
To say in his typical
Bold but jovial style,
"I know I just got here and all,
But I would appreciate you taking
Extra good care of my friend the Guvnor
And his wife as they serve you in Africa.
You know who I mean—
We've discussed them before.
Thanks, God.
I'm counting on it."

SEEING JESUS; BEING JESUS

Truly I tell you,

Whatever you did for one of the least

of these brothers and sisters of mine,

You did for me.

~Jesus

(Matthew 25:40 NIV)

THE BEGGAR OF PLAYA ICACOS

Can you see him reaching
with arms not there?
Can you feel him grasping
with hands jutting from shoulders?
Can you smell whiskey
wet on withered lips?
Can you hear his wounded heart
humming the blues?
Can you taste tears
trickling onto cardboard bed?
Can you conceive of life
without legs?
Can I give or will someone
Take it all from him?
Is a smile and kind word
of any value at all?
Where are his friends,
the ones who will carry him to Jesus?

I SEE CHILDREN

I see children, happy children
Basking in the golden sun
Playing games and making music
To the beating of the drums

I see children, shining children
Dressed for lessons in their school
Eager learners keen and hopeful
Poised to learn with books and tools

I see children being children
Just like children anywhere
But their stomachs ache with hunger
And their hearts break with despair

I see children, smiling children
Sitting in a darkened room
Light from windows and their faces
Dispel shadows, doubt and gloom

I see children, priceless treasures
Precious to our God above
Far removed from me by distance
Bound to me by Jesus' love

UGANDA, MY LOVELY

Uganda, my lovely eternal friend,
Those who don't know you cannot comprehend
The love that compels me oft to return-
Love from the Father for whom your heart yearns.

Clad in affluence, both hidden and seen
Natural, spiritual; wild and serene,
Your people and land by poverty scarred
Are humbled by burdens too harsh, too hard.

Voices of orphans with few choices stream;
 A poor, ragtag chorus rich in its dreams
Teeming with life, energy, and spirit
Their hearts, like drums, beat a rhythm; I hear it!

Your sights entice: jungle, bluff, lake, Nile's mouth;
Red fertile earth east to west, north to south.
Aromas of sweat, damp soil, charcoal fire;
Toil-infused air, life and death inspired.

No matter how long I must be away
No matter the distance my feet may stray
You still are my lovely young ancient girl;
Fairest of gems, the African pearl...Uganda!

THE BABY I CAN'T FORGET

Children darting, running, shouting, hanging onto me.
There in the dirt he sits —
Naked baby. Filthy naked baby —arms reaching, eyes locked on mine.

Shaking off the others I stoop, pull him to my chest —never mind my white blouse.
A tiny black hand grips my neck; his head finds my shoulder.
All of him melts into me as eyes close, breathing slows.

A full hour passes —an hour of whispered I love yous.

Tears course down my cheeks:
Tears for tomorrows when no one is here to cradle him;
For the others lying about in the dirt, flies pestering them.

I cry out to God, "How can this be? Where's the justice? Why do you allow it?"

The child wakes, coos, touches my face, reaches for the dirt.
A kiss goodbye and then I am washing up for a dinner I cannot eat.
What as my high, today? Holding a baby. My low? A filthy naked baby.

Later, much later I fumble through fragile, oft' fingered pages and
Find the words I know so well, but need to see for myself...for him:
"Whatever you did for the least of these you did for me."

HELPLESSNESS

Lying in bed on the third floor-
All is quiet but for a rooster crowing
And oldies playing in the courtyard,
Which seems odd on this continent
Half a world away from my own.

My senses are overloaded
...Inhale. Exhale. Pray. Relax...
So many needs, so much on my mind.
Scenes of poverty, sickness, starvation
Haunt me; tug me in all directions.

Screams! Screams of a child
Pierce the evening and the silence;
Terror fraught screams, volume increasing,
Punctuated by booming male voice
And whipping sounds ...and Incessant horrific screaming.

Racing to the balcony I look
Out, out, over the town.
Nothing. No movement.
No one rushing to the rescue...or caring...
Or even curious. Nothing.

I want to do something;
Run up and down the streets
Searching furiously until
I find the right house where so much is wrong;
I want to stop the beating. Stop the pain.
Take that screaming child far, far away...

But I, a mzungu, must not interfere
With the accepted order of things
Such as the routine beating
Of dogs, women, children on this continent
Half a world away from my own.

CULTURE SHOCK

I expected to meet
Starving children in Africa.
I expected to meet
People dying of AIDS.
I expected astonishing
Tales of survival
From civil wars, famines
And cattle raids.

I found all of these
Just as I had suspected,
Considered what remedies
I could employ.
Oh, I was prepared
To deal with their suffering.
I wasn't prepared
To deal with their joy.

YEARNING TO RETURN

O fly me to the land of crested crane
Of birds from every feather, every hue
Where herds of kob roam on the open plain
And monkey chatter pours from trees like rain

Show me her fields of sugar cane and maize
Her patchwork tea plantations in the hills
Her produce markets' colorful displays
The equal length of all her nights and days

Don't let me miss the falls at Mount Elgon
Or how Victoria Lake spews River Nile
Safaris starting at the crack of dawn
Beauteous landscapes stretching on and on

I can't forget her people gentle, mild
Yet joyful, passionate, hard working too
From esteemed elder to the orphan child
Their worship, song and dance has me beguiled

Africa's pearl I never thought I'd see
But when at last I had the chance I came
And oft' return because she calls to me
Like wood shrikes from an old acacia tree

STREET PRAYERS

I really don't belong here;
I'm not like all the others.
I used to be a football star just like my older brothers.
I once lived in a mansion with my rich and pretty wife
Until three men accosted me and tried to take my life.

God bless you for your kindness
And won't you say a prayer?
Living on the street like this
Is more than I can bear.

My belly's getting heavy
And it's hard to sleep at night.
Lying on this pavement just doesn't seem quite right.
I want to give my children a mother and a home.
This child will be my fourth, yet still I'll be alone.

God bless you for your kindness
And won't you say a prayer?
Living on the street like this
Is more than I can bear.

I don't want your charity;
It's work I'm looking for.
They learn that I'm a felon and won't let me in the door.
I don't need much to make it — fifty bucks a day or so.
If I'm hired, I'll stay sober. It won't be hard I know.

God bless you for your kindness
And won't you say a prayer?
Living on the street like this
Is more than I can bear.

IRON CLAD TRUTH

We humans are plentiful
And common as a populace.
Though we have many
Desirable qualities
Strength isn't our greatest asset;
But being connected –
In community, in relationship –
Strengthens us like nothing else.
Weakness make us vulnerable,
But hardship begets resilience.
Feet to the fire
We become pliable;
It is there, at our most vulnerable
That those who have been similarly
Challenged shape and
Encourage us to be everything
Our Master Craftsman intended.
Iron sharpens Iron;
One person sharpens another.

(Based on Proverbs 27:17)

FAMILY REDEFINED

I am part of a family- a large, unusual family.
Our members come from many countries
And speak in many tongues.
We don't dress alike,
Look alike,
Think alike,
Worship alike,
Or eat alike.
But each day we come together
To learn,
To play,
To celebrate,
To share victories,
To mourn losses.

When I began teaching refugees
I didn't know I was joining a family.
I already have a family –one that lives nearby;
One that speaks English,
Looks like me,
Dresses like me,
Worships like me.
I wasn't looking for a family.

But my new friends remind me most every day
In both subtle and outspoken ways that they left
Their families,
Their villages,
Their homes,
Their occupations,
All that is familiar and comfortable.
And we –teachers and students of their precious school –
Are family now for better or worse.
When terrible or amazing things
Happen to them –or to those they left behind...
When their village Is destroyed;
When a family member dies "back home";
When they make a scary trip to the hospital;
When they speak a full sentence in English,
Ace a spelling test,
Land a job,
Become an American citizen.

(continued)

My unique family
Makes me laugh, makes me cry,
Makes me worry, makes me pray.
They give me gifts –
Some lavish, Some touching in Their simplicity.
I wonder at their tenacity;
Marvel at their strength;
Admire their joy.

I love this family.
I am enriched by their differences
And blessed by their expressions
Of love and acceptance.
And though I don't feel worthy of inclusion,
I am better for being part of this
Large, unusual family.

TAG! YOU'RE WHO?

I peruse the name tag of each new arrival
Zohal, Horia, Fikri and Haval,
Nyankuet, Ayak, and Wongalwit—
These names don't roll off my tongue one bit.

Rama, Azel, Yananaeh, Mayar—
My students live here, though they came from afar.
Htoo May Moo, Asaph, and Paw Kblah Wah,
Shee Nay, Tha Hlei, and of course Abdullah.

There's Sincere (who is) and Silent (who's not)
Happy, Hosanna, Holy, and Dot.
Bethlehem, Glory, Magnolia, Iris,
Mohammad (times three), Sham, Ali and Frances.

With fifty plus students and name tags in all
I must get them right, so they'll come when I call.
So, I study each child and make it a game
To match up some aspect of them with their name.

Nametags aren't an option; they are critical.
Twins Aven and Vian dress identical!
And I, of course, wear a name tag too.
But for now, "Teacha! Teacha!" will have to do.

BLOSSOM

From her house on Lainson she pedaled every day,
Calling out to children she passed along the way.
Her plumpish form sat perched on a fendered yellow bike—
The basket filled with flowers, found treasures, and the like.

Her manner was quite odd, though no one seemed to care
That she was clamorous and wore daisies in her hair.
She was the rare adult who paid kids any mind;
Peculiar in most every way yet harmless, sure, and kind.

Her blouses were flamboyant with patterns bright and bold;
Her pants were usually striped or plaid if the truth is told.
But Blossom left a legacy as unique as her name
And up and down Harrison Street they still speak of her fame.

A PRAYER AND A PROMISE

Father full of mercy,
Jesus full of grace,
Hold us through this long, dark night
we yearn for your embrace.
Spirit, grant us comfort
in these dreadful hours.
Ragged pieces of our hearts
lie strewn about, like flowers
wilting in their frailty,
crushed beneath the tread
wishing time would turn around,
while it moves on instead.
Stunned by the violence,
staggering with grief,
we look to You for answers
and plead for some relief.
Hows and whys still haunt us.
Your word is undefiled—
You see the little sparrow fall,
How much more this child?

SINCE I SAW YOU LAST

Saw the corners of your eyes crinkle as our eyes met
Saw them moisten when you spoke of her
Saw the gray in your hair; wood shavings in your beard
Saw, scotch taped to the wall, memories —yellowed, curled,
Frayed from frequent fingering

Since I saw you last

Saw how the light had left your eyes
Saw how your lips quivered at goodbye
Saw how much and how little we each understood
Saw in dust filled beam your silhouette
Leaned against the doorjamb

Since I saw you last

I cry for you
I cry for her
I cry for anguished hopes and dreams
I cry for years that separate, beliefs that collide
For prayers yet to be answered
Hovering between heaven and earth

Since I saw you last

A PRAYER IN THE WITCHING HOUR

Where are You, God?

Shadows submerge me in darkness. Gloom enshrouds me like a grave. It is the witching hour and the presence of evil is great. Where is Your Goodness? Heavy, my eyelids close. But sleep eludes me. The pallet is too hard, and I miss my pillow.

Where are You, God?

Today I walked strange paths, lined with unfamiliar sights. People pressed against me, people whose manner and odor were strong. I peered into gaunt faces with toothless smiles. Questioning eyes stalked me. Children pointed and giggled as I passed. Adults touched my pale skin and stroked my silky hair. Uncertain, I continued in silence, fearful of committing a cultural sin or murdering their native tongue.

Where are You, God?

My perceptions are keen, but You are remote. I search for a glimpse of Your beauty but see only squalor. Where is your fragrance? These streets reek of urine. Your voice is drowned by distant drums rumbling to placate the demons. I cannot feel Your arms around me.

Where are You, God?

I heeded Your call and followed You here. You should be nearer than ever before, but You are absent. How will I speak unless Your Spirit speaks through me? How will I serve without your strength to hold me up? How will I love unless You love through me? How will I live without Your presence?

Where are You, God?

I found you as a child. Your grace brought me through trials. Your Spirit overflowed in the prayer meeting where I met the aging missionary. Your joy surged through me when I promised to come to this distant land. Not until now have I doubted. Was I duped? Deceived?

Where are You, God?

I didn't know that I would feel so insignificant and out of place. I didn't know that I would ache to hear my family's voices. I didn't know that I would feel repulsed by the very people I came to serve. I didn't know that nighttime could be this dark or this lonely. I didn't know that You could be so elusive.

Where are You, God?

(continued)

"Search me, O God, and know my heart; test me and know my anxious thoughts. See if there is any offensive way in me and lead me in the way everlasting." (Psalm 139:23-24 NIV)

Where are You, God?

You are in the loneliness, the stench, the unfamiliarity, the darkness, the silence. Slay my selfishness. Forgive my unbelief. Dispel my doubts. Quell my fears. Fill this jar of clay. Then, "I will lie down and sleep in peace, for you alone, O LORD, make me dwell in safety." (Psalm 4:8 NIV)

DISGUISED

I have befriended foreigners
From war-torn homelands
Who fear for their safety
Here in the land of the free.

I have cradled babies
With deep set hollowed eyes
Bellies like balloons
And sticks for legs.

I have visited women
In prison- debtors
Who pay in daily misery
And decimated futures

I have given water to men
Laboring in the sun
Sweat flowing from every pore-
Flogged for stopping to drink.

I have bathed orphans,
Replacing rags
With homemade dresses,
Grime with gap-toothed grins.

I have bought medicine to ease
A dying woman's pain;
And more to cure
Her orphaned daughter.

For behind the facade of
Sickness, grime, rags, chains,
Bloated bellies, and strangers
I saw Jesus.

LOVE AND ROMANCE

I do not know

Whether it is better to love deeply

Or to be deeply loved.

I only know the weakness in my knees

When we touch.

I BELIEVE YOU STILL

When you said, "I love you"
So many years ago
Before the story of us
Had begun to unfold
Some thought it foolish of me
To believe you.
But for that look in your eyes
I might have hesitated.

And now, after all these years
When I catch you
Gazing across the table
With those same
Lovesick puppy eyes,
My heart swells
With the numerous ways
You have loved me well and…

I believe you still.

ALL SHOOK UP AT THE HOP

I'd spoken to her many times.
We'd had a casual date.
Every time I saw that girl
My heart would palpitate.

She was a gorgeous cheerleader
And I was just Joe Schmuck.
I feared approaching her again
Would really push my luck.

And yet here was my opening;
It seemed the perfect chance.
I offered to escort her to
Our college Fifties Dance.

Great beads of perspiration
Upon my brow arose.
Shrugging, she replied with
A resounding, "I suppose."

My heart did several flip-flops.
I was thrilled beyond belief.
"Stay cool," my ego whispered
As I trembled with relief.

A prize was being offered
For the couple dressed the best.
I found the perfect get-up.
I knew she'd be impressed.

Saddle shoes and poodle skirt
Bedecked my Sally Jean,
Plus a curve-enhancing sweater
And a scarf in kelly green.

She called my broken glasses
Taped together with a wad
A crazy stroke of genius.
Whew! What an act of God!

(continued)

With confidence and valor
I took her by the hand,
Then turned and twirled and spun her
To the be-bop of the band.

My rhythm was atrocious.
I could not keep the beat;
So I tried to keep her moving
Without stepping on her feet."

We twisted, shook and shimmied
'Til the final song was played;
Then caught our breath and waited
As the costumes were assayed.

"Eight finalists were chosen,"
Said the judge who held the page.
I beamed at Sally Jean as
We were called up to the stage.

"The winner," he continued,
Is really quite a clown.
While he has been up dancing,
His zipper has been down."

In haste my eyes averted.
How I prayed it wasn't me!
Then I glimpsed my whitey-titeys.
What a grim catastrophe!

My trembling fingers fumbled.
The crowd —how it did roar!
I wished that I could disappear
Or melt into the floor.

My blood was surging upward
In a retroactive rush.
It set my heart to pounding,
Made my whole complexion flush.

(continued)

At last my pants were fastened,
And I peered at Sally Jean.
She grabbed my hand and flashed the
Biggest smile I'd ever seen.

"We won! We get two tickets
To the big concert next week!"
She squealed, and then she planted
A wet kiss upon my cheek.

Another date with Sally?
My head began to whirl.
I'd take being embarrassed
If it meant I got the girl.

NOTE: Joe and Sally Jean (Johnson) Schmuck have celebrated over forty years of marriage. Although Joe's sense of rhythm has not improved, his philosophy, "Keep her dancing, without stepping on her toes," suits Sally just fine. Joe and Sally's names have been changed to protect...well, you've probably figured it out by now!

TRUE LOVE, YOU AND ME LOVE

Reflecting back upon the day
When first I learned your name;
A day when love was nothing more
Than just a silly game;
How far we've come since first we met
And how we two have changed;
Our lives so separate, so remote,
Now greatly rearranged.
Now I find my greatest joy
In filling your desire;
My heart unfolding like a flower
To all your love inspires.
I see my love reflected
In the smile upon your face,
And I realize that what we share
Is far from commonplace.

UNITY

I spoke your name
With my first waking breath.
As I stretched my arms,
I felt yours caressing me.
I stepped into a new day and
Knew it would hold meaning...
Because of you.

My Love,
Only these many miles can separate us.
For I am still with you
And you with me every moment,
Even though we are apart.
This is the meaning of unity...
Though we are separate,
We are one.

YOUR HANDS SPEAK LOVE

Your hands speak love
In words not made of sounds
But heard with heart, not ears,
where love abounds.

They nimbly pluck
My heart's eternal strings
evoking songs as sweet
as warblers sing.

Work roughened hands
Create, they toil and wear;
Then capably enfold,
Caress, and care;

And capture this,
My longing and design:
My hands with yours shall
Ever be entwined.

ONE MOMENT

There was a moment long ago,
'Tis with me now, the same.
How long? You ask.
I do not know—
An age and yet a day.
My longing heart would have me
Living in that moment still,
And in my dreams I sense
That again someday I will
Be caught up in that moment
And it will go on and on.
One moment, yet it lends the strength
I need for all the rest.
Time stands stubbornly between
That moment and the next.

DAILY HABIT

"Keys, badge, lunch, kiss,"
Patting pocket, pail, and pouch-
Leaning in with puckered lips-
Daily ritual recited
At precisely half past six.

Nothing brilliant, I suppose.
Still, our kiss is named among
The things he never leaves without.
If I can always count on that,
Certainly, I can count on him.

MY DAY FRIDAY

Friday is my day
My day to sleep
Sip coffee
Birdwatch

Friday is my day
My day to garden
Write
Play with Kitty.

Friday is my day
My day to regroup
Refresh
Rekindle love

And best of all...

Friday night is our night
Date night
Stay out late night
Yours and mine.

MORE THAN A VALENTINE

I awake in the morning and glimpse first of all
A ghastly reflection in the mirror on the wall.
You kiss me and don't even mention
That my face could use some attention.
You pretend that I look (and smell) just fine—
You're so much more than a valentine!

I go to the kitchen and discover the dishes
Have been put away, fulfilling my wishes.
The garbage has been taken care of
As one more token of your love.
You've even left food so my cats can dine—
You're so much more than a valentine!

You never complain if the food isn't great
And you'll fend for yourself if I'm running late.
In almost any instance
I can count on you for assistance.
If I ask, you rarely decline—
You're so much more than a valentine!

You know how to give good gifts from the heart.
You make special days a blast from the start.
The fun element of surprise
Is often revealed in your eyes;
When you're up to something, they dance and shine—
You're so much more than a valentine!

You kiss and caress me whenever you can.
I tell you my secrets, my dreams and my plans.
If I'm sad you understand,
You hug me and hold my hand.
Your affection toward me is divine—
You're so much more than a valentine!

Most things that we do, we do as a team.
Being your wife is almost like a dream.
The memories we create
I simply can't over-rate.
Our talents and traits perfectly combine.
You're so much more than a valentine!

FOR THE LOVE OF COFFEE

A bold aroma
wafts
from somewhere
down the hall
curling
swirling into nostrils
causing sleepy eyes to
flutter open

No husband
on my left
where pillows mound
in jumble of covers

A-hah!
I grin as realization
mingles with
olfactory sensation

How clever of him
brewing
coffee
as a way of speaking
willing
my senses
to awaken
the rest of me

Inhaling
I hear him
express
silently, boldly
the depths of
his love
his desire
to share the morning with me

Yawn...
I roll right to
gleaming smile
beaming down

(continued)

His presence warms
my being
as steaming cup
draws me up

Setting cup aside
he bends
sends flutters
through me
with his lips

Who needs caffeine?

Ardent kisses granted
I must admit I do

70 YEAR PORTRAIT OF A MAARRIAGE

On that day in 1948
A day of firsts...
First day of January,
First day of a new year,
First day of life as one,
First day of a long, long journey...

On that day in 1948
You couldn't have known
That your journey would last
839 months, 3,650 weeks,
25,500 days, 613,200 hours,
36,792,000 minutes, and 2,207,520,000 Seconds.

You wouldn't have known
That you would produce three children,
Who in turn would produce grandchildren,
And that they in turn would produce great grandchildren.
You couldn't have imagined all the places you would go,
The homes in which you would live,
The friends you would make along the way.

Oh, I know it wasn't always easy.
You had your moments, your days, your weeks, your years
When needs were great and money tight.
When the two of you didn't quite see eye to eye.
(I glimpsed more than a few eye rolls and heard
Many a sigh by Barbara in response to Jerry's antics!)

But your promises made were promises kept
For better or worse, richer or poorer, in sickness and health.
And forsaking all others you clung to God, to marriage, to each other.
For many of us your marriage has become
The one we observed the longest.
And it makes us smile and sigh; delights us;
Points us to the One who holds life-worn hearts together;
Makes us believe in happily ever-afters.

Because you helped us see marriage
As something worth pursuing,
Something worth fighting for,
Something beautiful, if not perfect,
But also, as a promise kept
So long as you both shall live.

LOVE BY COMPARISON

When love was new and every day had its firsts
I hoped it might stay like that forever...
Living to be surprised, to discover,
To attempt to satisfy all love's hungers and thirsts.

Over time love has become comfortable –
More deeply satisfying than ever
Like my favorite flannel shirt that never
Bunches, pinches, or disappoints –incomparable.

FAMILY

Family glue is mostly sweat and tears;

And love is measured

By moments and breaths,

Not years.

WISH UPON A WILLOW

The tree I imagined reflecting from our pond
Was the willow of other poets' poems,
Gentle breeze whispering through her skirts
Rustling just above the grass
For inspiration.

The tree that grew there instead
Is a monstrous willow that never weeps,
But carelessly strews its brittle branches
Across the lawn making more work
For me.

It is a bit like raising children, I suppose:
For all your imagination and dreams
They make messes and become what they will,
While perfect willows grow across the way
For comparison.

But beneath my willow are gaggles of geese
Shade for picnics, children swinging
And a hammock for dreaming.
Who would trade all that living
For weeping?

HOUSE RULES

Whosoever visits this home shall be welcomed...wholeheartedly.
Whosoever is offered food shall accept or refuse...graciously.
Whosoever eats at the table shall observe their manners...politely
Whosoever spills shall wipe it up...immediately.
Whosoever opens a door shall close it...gently.
Whosoever uses the toilet shall flush it...promptly.
Whosoever flushes shall wash their hands...thoroughly.
Whosoever plays games shall do so...honestly.
Whosoever wins or loses shall accept it...humbly.
Whosoever plays, works, converses, or makes music shall do it...joyfully.
Whosoever runs amok in Grandma's garden...seriously?
Whosoever makes sudden loud noises near Papa...just don't.
Whosoever plays with toys shall put them away...neatly.
Whosoever arrives empty shall leave filled...abundantly.

FIRSTBORN

A son...our firstborn...fragile, yet strong.
Wisps of red hair frame his small Gerber face.
This gift from above we awaited so long;
Now alive and complete, he resists our embrace!
We are so young and know so little of
How to fulfill his desires and needs.
We ask for wisdom, patience and love.
We desire to teach not with words, but with deeds.
Who is this child? What will he become?
A person emerges as days turn to weeks.
He's training us slowly. We're teaching him some.
Our full attention he constantly seeks.
We watch, mesmerized, every move that he makes.
He's agile, determined, and stubborn perhaps.
Neither cuddling nor pacifiers soothe when he wakes.
Only motion and music (quite loud) make him nap.
As weeks turn to months it's becoming quite clear
This boy achieves all he aspires to do.
Now it's hard to recall life before he was here;
And we love him so much we don't ever wish to!

MASTER OF THE MIDDLE

Forty years ago you were born our second son.
Two years after that you became the middle one.
You strove to feel significant; yes, this much is true.
With a brother on each side you soon became the glue.

You're the plot of the story; the meat of the nuts;
To an orange the navel, and to an engine guts;
The mezzo, moderato, a bridge between two shores;
The median of the boulevard; the chocolate in my s'mores.

The bullseye of the target, the square of the town;
The polis of the metro, my pillow's feathery down.
Never just the donut's hole, you were something more—
The jelly in my bismark, the heart, the hub, the core;

In short the middle is the space that only you can fill.
As the Master of the Middle I see and love you still.

DIMPLED DAYDREAMER

His puppy-dog eyes and dimpled chin
Could cave this mother's heart right in;
But he wasn't aware they did so.

He sang contentedly as he played;
Held stuffed animal class each day;
Where his big brothers went, he'd follow.

His eye for detail and his talent for art
Are some of the traits that set him apart;
His work was careful and quite slow.

Although in school he often daydreamed
His memory was vast, his verbiage extreme.
He could spout facts we did not know.

He teaches and builds with expert skill;
He plays guitar, and writes music, still;
Pores over books most would forego.

His Father in Heaven holds him so dear
He gave him a heart sensitive and sincere.
We've been blessed to see this son grow.

TO YOU, MY DAUGHTERS IN LAW AND LOVE

Have I told you how I longed for the day you would join our family;
Longed for females to tame our all male clan;
Longed to chat, plan, plot, and shop with you?
If not, I'm telling you now.

Have I told you how thankful I am that God introduced you to our son;
That our son, in turn, introduced you to us;
That you said, "Yes" when he asked for your hand?
If not, I'm telling you now.

Have I told you that I loved you from the very first time we met;
Loved you because our son chose you;
Loved you because I trusted his heart?
If not, I'm telling you now.

Have I told you that I prayed for you even before I knew you;
Before I knew that you were the one;
Before you completed him so well?
If not, I'm telling you now.

Have I told you how thankful I am that you are mom to his children;
Mom to our grandchildren;
Mom magnificent, extraordinaire?
If not, I'm telling you now.

Have I told you that I have come to like you as much as I love you;
Admire the traits nurtured in you;
Admire the unique qualities you have honed?
If not, I'm telling you now.

Have I told you I respect how you fulfill your roles of wife and mother;
Respect your godly maternal wisdom;
Value you for freely sharing your family with us?
If not, I'm telling you now.

Have I told you that I often pray that your marriage will endure;
That your love for each other will continue and grow;
That your marriage will point others to Christ?
If not, I'm telling you now.

SWEET BABY

Sweet baby, I don't know your name;
but sometimes I think that I may know your face.
Dreamily I recall the day your daddy was born
...eight perfect pounds of little boy
with rounded cheeks and fuzz for hair.
Grasping my fingers tightly in his little fist,
he rendered my heart defenseless.
But mine wasn't the only one!
Soon we learned that he could melt hearts
As quickly as a summer day melts ice cream.
Born an entertainer, your daddy was both dramatic and humorous.
Feigning "owies" or sleep, he often inspired laughter.
He hated being alone; perhaps because he rarely was.
Two brothers, one older and one younger, made him the middle child.
Your daddy still feels out of place if he isn't in the middle!
Compassion, kindness, faith and joy;
these were etched on that little face—
the one I glimpsed for the first time twenty-seven years ago.
Will your face mirror your daddy's winsome face,
or will you have your mommy's lovely eyes and dainty nose?
It doesn't matter either way! I love you just the same.

A METAMORPHOSIS

A voice comes from behind me
Familiar yet unknown.
I turn to see a boy I've loved since birth
Much taller grown.
His eyes hold the same luster
But now his jaw is square.
Above his upper lip and on his legs and arms
There's hair.

This boy I used to cuddle,
Who bounced upon my knee,
Is stretching upward day by day and soon
May pass up me.
His hair normally tousled
Now sports a teenage style—
Highlighted curls that complement his
Orthodontic smile.

I pause now for reflection
On thirteen years flown fast,
Grateful I can be part of his present
And his past
Not only as his grandma
But first teacher as well.
So many times he's awed us; in so many ways
Excelled.

Most precious was he always;
Most precious he will stay.
I pray he makes wise choices
as he goes
From day to day.

My prayers go ever with him
I am his greatest fan
Whether darling little boy or
Emergent young man.

TREMORS

Something awakened me:
a rattling, shaking sound
unidentifiable.
"Do you hear it?" I asked,
jiggling his arm.
"It's nothing," he said.
But twice more it came;
a quiet rustling
growing in
strength and volume
before subsiding again.
It was all the buzz
in the morning-
earthquake in the heartland
felt for miles.
I knew
it was something extraordinary
in those early hours
of April eighteenth—
the morning after Claire Carleta,
who continues to rock our world,
made her debut.

ALL THIS AND MORE

Star...
Beaming, gleaming,
Commanding your audience

Doll...
Girly, twirly
Curly locks springing like coils

Dream...
Surreal, ethereal,
Air-like aura about you

Chatterbox...
Taking charge
Freely giving your opinion

Ham...
Plucky, poised,
A noisy merrymaker

Sugar...
Delightful, sweet,
Cannot get enough of you

Jewel...
Priceless, rare,
Sparkly granddaughter of mine

MIXTURE OF SWEETNESS

A barrel of kindness
A bushel of love
A bundle of energy
Sent from above
A cup of sweetness
A scoop of tease
A sprinkle of freckles...
Combine all of these
Then stir in adventure
Curiosity
A passion for books
For dirt plants and trees
Allow this mixture
To grow and to gel
And soon you'll behold
Our gentle yet passionate
Always compassionate
Selah Noel.

I AM ME

I am Josie Jean LaRue.
Do you know what I can do?
I can be a princess or a queen.
I love to dance and spin
Play dress-up and pretend.
May I serve you up some cake and tea?

You will rarely see me wear
The same outfit anywhere;
I may sport a boa, gown, or wings.
With my tiara a-tilt
My high heels add to my lilt
When I sing the songs I love to sing.

I am sweet and I am kind
But I also know my mind.
If you cross me you will rue the day!
My brother and my sis
Will surely tell you this;
Though they both adore me anyway!

HOPE

Hope, the meaning of your name
Is more than whimsy or a game;
More than childish fantasy
Or wishing well frivolity.

Hope from God is better far
Than pot of gold or falling star.
It's an anchor -safe, secure-
A place to stand when life's unsure.

Where God's love and truth abound
A quiet confidence is found
Giving reason to expect
What nobody has seen just yet.

Hope lifts eyes to Heaven above;
Assures us of our Savior's love;
Keeps your feet from stumbling
When things around are crumbling.

On with life, a "hoper" goes;
Needn't cross fingers or toes;
Waits with patience and with peace
As confidence and joy increase.

Hope won't disappoint, you know;
Your mom and dad have found it so.
Sweet child, your parents hoped for you.
God answered, and their dreams came true.

A GIFT THAT KEEPS ON GIVING

A robust miracle with lots of hair
Prayed for, longed for,
Loved for so long before
She made her appearance—
A highly anticipated birth.

That baby grew...

Intelligent, impish, imaginative...
The girl knows her own mind
And loves spending time
With cousins, friends,
Or anyone game for pretending.

Her specialties...

Party planner, instigator,
Enthusiastic participator—
Olive is all of these.
Drawings, bear hugs, and love notes:
These are treasures she generously shares.

OUR BROWN EYED GIRL

Magnificent brown eyes warmly inviting
Catcher of moonbeams rays from the sun
You mesmerize delight in delighting
Hold captive enlighten instigate fun

Mysterious brown eyes puddles of wonder
Concealers of secrets revealers of charm
You mastermind strategize create ponder
Unworried unhurried amaze and disarm

Mischievous brown eyes known to bedazzle
Courageous in battle contagious in wit
You masquerade as we strive to unravel
Whether felon or hero inspires your grit

SOMETHING ABOUT THIS BOY

He is our tail-end book-end
Our bespectacled young friend
Last of the eight grandchildren
From the two of us to descend.

My, but this boy is curious;
His play— fast and furious
As Batman, cheetah or ape
And others just as precarious

Keeping us all on our toes
We follow him as he goes
Telling his thoughts as he thinks them
In humorous whimsical prose.

This boy, though gangly and bony
Gobbles up macaroni,
Salad, grilled cheese, and grapes
And not at Grandma's house only.

Strange how this little boy's charm
Can often serve to disarm
His mostly unbiased grandmother
When he cuddles right up in her arms.

ENDOWED MEMORY

A frilly handkerchief, my dear,
like my Grandma's before Kleenex.
We cuddled in church
like you and me.

Watch its magic...

Match the corners,
forming a triangle.
Roll from each point
to the center
along the folded edge,
both rolls meeting in the center.
Peel into two the remaining point,
forming a cradle out and around
the "twin babies"
bundled inside.
Pinch each corner
and rock the babies
to your heart's content.

Its real magic?

Connecting five generations-
Enfolding you and me, my darling,
tying you to Great Great Grandma
smiling from Heaven.

GARDEN SECRET

Lift the latch,
Swing open the gate.
Place her hand in mine.

Leap the marigolds,
Tiptoe 'round cabbages
Kneel in damp earth
Beside rows of lettuces.

Wrap her hand around the leaves;
Cut the stems,
Eyes locked on hers.

Watch a leaf
Find her mouth
Grinning, enticing…
We both indulge.

Plump radish protrudes
Scarlet and white.
Rock 'til it lets go,
Cheering each conquest.

Pink raspberries
Play hide and seek.
We eat every. last. one.

Now for the peas.
I pull a dangling pod,
Split it and pop
Four small orbs into her hand.

"Uh-uh" she says,
Shaking her head,
But one rolls round and round
Landing on her tongue.

Crunch. Swallow.
"I don't like peas,
But I like these," She says.

We pick a mess,
Podding a few
To munch as we go.

(continued)

Then back to the gate
Past the zucchini
Where a friendly toad
Sits blinking at the sun.

Leap the marigolds,
Re-latch the gate.
And off she skips,
Pail of peas and lettuces swinging.

Back inside
Her chatter consists
Of garden sights,
Tastes, and sounds.

But her newfound
Fondness for peas—
Remains a secret kept.

VIOLETS ON HER WINDOWSILL

Pinching pennies, making do,
Scrimping here, and saving, too;
Just necessities were bought.
Luxuries were rarely sought.
Mother chose the simple thrill
Of violets on her window sill.

Picking spinach, podding peas,
Sewing patches for my knees,
Cutting noodles, kneading bread,
Braiding hair, keeping us fed—
Mother did all this and still
Grew violets on her window sill.

Once, when I was nearly grown
Mother let me stay alone;
Took a trip, left me in charge.
Wow! I learned her shoes were large.
Instructions seemed routine until
We reached the kitchen window sill.

"While I'm gone take care of these.
Don't get water on their leaves.
Fill the saucer, not the pot.
Too much, and their roots will rot.
Please be careful not to kill
The violets on my window sill."

Cooking, cleaning, scrubbing floors,
Doing laundry, locking doors,
Kept me busy, ripened me,
Taught responsibility.
And I honed the proper skill
For violets on the window sill.

As I grew I thought of ways
I would rather spend my days.
When a home and kids I got,
Like my mother I was not.
I had no desire or will
For violets on my window sill.

(continued)

Years and decades soon had passed.
Life was full and much too fast.
Then my mother -active, strong-
Sensed something was very wrong.
I tended her while she was ill,
And the violets on her sill.

Soon, her final days were spent.
To her heavenly home she went.
Still, five purple blooms remained,
And a fondness I had gained.
So, I've resolved I finally will
Grow violets on my window sill.

MAMA'S SEWING MACHINE

It woke me in the morning
and hummed throughout my dreams,
the rat-a-tat-a-tat of
Mama's sewing machine.

As I dressed my dollies or
built castles out of blocks
Mama's skillful fingers sewed
my dainty little frocks.

She'd start by pinning patterns
to fabric underneath.
I'd hear her mumbling to me
with pins between her teeth.

Then armed with gleaming scissors
or else with pinking shears,
a rhythmic chomping sounded
like music in my ears.

I wondered how she knew where
to make her marks with chalk.
I'd snatch a piece for scrawling
stick people on the walk.

Removal of the pattern
provoked a tiny doubt.
*Why was she now re-pinning
the fabric inside out?*

Next came the tat-tat-tatter
as piece was stitched to piece,
and then each seam was ironed
to emphasize the crease.

As she sewed, I dumped her tin
of buttons on the floor;
then sorted piles of colors
around me on the floor.

I stuffed the buttons in my socks
and shook them as I ran,
adding my percussion to
her rat-a-tat-a-tan.

(continued)

When time came for my fitting
I sucked in all my breath.
Sharp pins threatened to poke me;
they scared me half to death.

I viewed with eyes bedazzled
the garment taking shape
with smocking on the bodice
and underskirt of crepe.

With rat-a-tat now finished,
her thimble Mama took
to blind-stitch 'round the hemline
and fasten eye and hook.

From yard goods to perfection
before my wondering eyes
a dress fit for a princess
hung finished in my size.

Throughout my days of childhood
and as a gangly teen
Mama's rat-a-tat-a-tat
accompanied every scene.

Sweet diaper sets for dollies
and dungarees for play,
pleated skirts for cheerleading
and clothes for everyday,

A fancy gown for prom night…
Would it evoke a kiss?
my dress for graduation
of pale blue dotted swiss.

She made clothing for travel
that took me 'round the world,
matched outfits for my bridesmaids
and giggly flower girls.

My Mama kept on sewing;
made PJ's for my boys,
three Easter suits of velvet
and teddy bears for toys.

(continued)

Her rat-a-tat-a-tat-a
continued through the years,
weaving tender memories
with sentimental tears.

One day she rang my doorbell
and much to my surprise,
a lovely quilt unfolded
amid astonished cries.

Joined in a four-heart pattern
lay pieces of my past.
It was her finest offering
and it would be her last.

Mama lives in Heaven now
and sometimes in my dreams
I see her sewing raiment
for the angels. How it gleams!

It's buried in my closet, her
Machine is silent now.
I'm not as skilled as Mama,
but she spurs me on, somehow.

And sensing Mama's presence
through the visions I have seen,
I begin to rat-a-tat on
Mama's sewing machine.

GEODES

I wasn't often invited
Into his garden
Or on his expeditions:
Berry picking, auctions, rock hunting.
Still I tagged along—
Wary of snakes and briar patches,
Trying hard to keep up.

My inquiries were mostly met
With silence or derision;
So, I never quite knew
What treasure he sought
Until he whooped and hollered
Over a treasure found.

And that is how I learned to
Persevere,
Be vigilant,
Value what's on the inside,
And envy geodes.

A SIMPLY WONDERFUL CHRISTMAS

I know it's Christmas because
My family has just arrived at Grandma's early this snowy evening.
A life-sized lit-up Santa stands in the neighbor's yard,
But Grandma's ornaments are simple and hand-made...
Mostly by her grandchildren.
The package I carry conceals a cake of soap that
I carved and beaded to look like a swan.
It doesn't smell as good as she does, I think,
As she greets me with her warm hug and familiar laughter.
I run to the kitchen to drink from the dipper
That hangs by her kitchen sink, just as it always has
Since the days she pumped water from her well.
Next, I check her peach-shaped cookie jar, finding
Soft raisin cookies and chewy date bars inside.
"Don't spoil your dinner, she chides,"
As she mounds her specialty —Cornflake Chicken —on a plate.
I am both flattered and a little frightened when she sends me to the cellar
To fetch a jar of fruit to eat later with the cookies.
Taking the lantern she has lit, I slowly make my way
Down the stairs that lie beneath her heavy cellar door.
Spiders scurry from the flickering light, sending shivers up my spine.
Rows and rows of jars line the shelves--
Fruit and vegetables grown and canned by Grandma.
She must know that I will choose pears, like always.
We gather 'round her table and bow our heads to bless the meal,
Squinting, I watch Grandma rub her forehead, as if doing so
Will seal and preserve each line to retrieve later, when she prays from her chair.
Dish washing water heats on the stove during dinner,
And after dishes are washed, dried, and put away
We all settle into her tiny living room while more water heats for baths.
I try to imagine Grandma's delight when she sees my gift to her;
But first she has one for me —this Grandma who scrimps and saves,
Recycles when it is unfashionable to do so,
And still works every day at the age of seventy-two
Has bought me, her youngest grandchild, a most exquisite gift—
A rose-patterned china tea set!
It takes my breath away.
My no-nonsense Grandma doesn't share my passion
For poetry, music, pretty trinkets or cats;
But she has always tolerated my incessant chatter.
And now I know that she heard. She cared.
She chose for me a gift I will forever treasure,
Just as I will forever cherish her...my strong, beautiful Grandma
And this simply wonderful Christmas.

THE WANDERLUST

He came loaded with treasures like I'd never seen—
Old toys, farm tools, music boxes, machines—
Smelling strongly of garlic and Listerine,
Exclaiming that I had grown like a bean.

In the back of his truck was a thick pile of hay.
His litter of puppies rode nicely that way—
English Shepherds for farmers willing to pay
Whatever he needed to make it that day.

He reached under the hay for his old mandolin
Then tucked in the pups before he came in.
O the music he played made my heart dance and spin
Though Mama had always said dancing was sin.

He wove yarns of strange far-off people and places;
Gave me dresses for dolls trimmed in elegant laces;
Scooped me up in his arms for some scratchy embraces;
Then bid us goodnight as he packed up his cases.

"He's an old junk dealer," his customers claim,
Though his card said "The Dog Man" under his name.
"You backslider, you!" I heard Grandma exclaim.
I just called him Grandpa each time that he came.

DOORS

I reminisce
and in the midst
of all that shimmers
are sisters
giddy, giggling,
mischievous mimickers,
silly, secretive,
sometimes including
me – impish baby sister-
invited in the side door

Kindred spirits
linked by lineage, image,
swapping shirts
sharing pizza, friends:
quibbling, indignantly
slamming doors
In a snit

Time ticks, sand sifts
shifting roles
dismantling, distancing
stretching, merging
through revolving doors
molding us into
older versions of ourselves
obvious images
of another—our mother

Three women
waltzed before me
facing calm, calamity;
gathering courage,
consequences
stumbling sometimes
opening doors
offering counsel-
solicited
or not

(continued)

Older, bolder
innocence spent
louder laughter and lament
partners found
Providence profound—
forever bond
forged with another
doors closed
that needed closing

Sisters stick together
-it's intended—
I wish it were
as true for four
as for three.
Some secrets construct
impervious walls
void of
doors, windows, cracks
even for sisters

One sticks
closer than a sister
knows sorrow
greater than ours
implores, inspires,
empowers, forgives,
frees hearts from
walls of stone,
opens Himself -the door—
seeks to restore
sisters

I AM FROM CALICO

I am from calico, from Ajax and the plains.

I am from simple, tidy, squeaky clean.

I am from wheat, sunflowers, corn;
        oak trees, African violets, and sunshine.

I am from gardening, canning and elbow grease;
        from Grandma Pearl, Willard and Bernice.

I am from legalism and talking without communicating
        From "a place for everything, and everything in its place."
        and "what will people think?"

I am from born-again, Bible-believing, regular church attendance;
        saved by, but unacquainted with, grace.

I am from Kansas, Nebraska, and Iowa- sweet corn, potatoes, bread and jelly;

From the misadventures of Anita, Dwanna, and Beth
        hitching goats to carts and milking them to feed me;
        and Grandpa, "The Dog Man," arriving
        with a truckload of junk and puppies.

I am from the basement, the closet, the photo albums and boxes
        crammed with mementos I rarely disturb
        lest memories resurrected return me
        to a place I long ago left behind.

EVERYONE NEEDS AN UNCLE JERRY

Everyone needs an Uncle Jerry
Who's quirky, witty, and a little scary;
And by that, I mean unpredictable,
For life with my uncle is never dull.

He lives impulsively, fully and free,
A friend to all with few enemies;
Yet never afraid to speak the truth
Regardless who's listening –elders or youth.

A lover of children, a lover of fun
Who would play, engage, and even run—
Adults like that are rare indeed;
My Uncle Jerry is a special breed.

While the kids were playing hide and seek
He would leave the adults and quietly sneak
Behind a corner, a bush or tree
And scare the bejeebers out of me!

And that's not all; because of him
I learned to roller skate, ice skate, and swim.
With his own kids I was often included
In many pursuits that might well have eluded.

I'd be remiss if I failed to mention
Jerry's love for bargains and wheelin' dealin'
Transactions are made anytime, anywhere
With a nod or a handshake –price fairer than fair.

Yes, everyone needs an Uncle Jerry
Full of zest, zeal, and laughter so merry
What a valuable gift; a treasure rare
A blessing in life who has always been there.

IT MIGHT BE A STRETCH
(a prose poem)

Grandma's hammock fits me just right. When Grandma climbs in and lets me push, the hammock fits her bigger, rounder body just right, too. Once, when Grandma was in the hammock, Grandpa crawled in beside her. They were so smushed together they couldn't stop giggling. I thought the hammock would burst, but it stretched to fit around them both.

"Grandma" is a stretchy word. In fact, I think it's a lot like a hammock. It doesn't matter who climbs in, it stretches to fit. Some words aren't very stretchy. If a bunch of people drew pictures of an apple or a baseball bat, their pictures would all look alike, but if they drew grandmas, their pictures would be very different.

Grandmas come in all shapes and sizes. They can be tall or short, thin or plump. Many grandmas play sports, ride bikes, or exercise, but some need a cane or walker just to cross the room. My great grandma shakes her cane at me when she means business. Some grandmas wear glasses, and some don't. Their hair can be long or short and can come in any color, with or without some gray hair mixed in.

Most grandmas enjoy taking their grandchildren for walks. They are good at noticing things like ant hills, robin's nests, and cats curled up in window sills. But grandmas might also drive you in their van, sports car, pick-up, or tractor. They sometimes ride motorcycles, horses, carousels, and roller coasters.

You never know where a grandma might pop up. She could be your teacher, your waitress, your doctor, your school bus driver, or your mail carrier. Some of your neighbors are probably grandmas, too. I'm pretty sure every grandma knows how to bake cookies, but I could be wrong about that.

Grandmas know all about little kids, because they had kids once. Just don't expect them to know your favorite cartoon characters. They have lots of toys stashed away in boxes, but the cars look funny, and some are missing important parts like wheels. Their dolls' pigtails have been chopped off, and they have lipstick stains on their faces. For some reason, Grandmas get teary eyed when they see you playing with those old toys. They don't care too much if you make a mess.

If you want to hear a great story, just climb into your grandma's lap and ask for one. My grandma's lap is as cushiony as a pillow, but your grandma's lap might not be so soft. Still, she probably knows "The Three Bears" and "The Three Little Pigs" by heart. She can tell you things that no one else knows about your daddy, and about all kinds of strange things she had as a little girl –like roller skates with keys, records bigger around than dinner plates, and black and white television sets without remotes. She will show you pictures of Grandpa with hair and a mustache, and your aunts and uncles in diapers.

(continued)

Grandmas make pretty good teachers, too. Some grandmas can teach you how to plant flowers. Others give music lessons on the piano or violin. Some grandmas are good at using tools, and they can help you learn to build or fix things. Lots of grandmas know how to sew, knit, or crochet. Maybe yours can teach you how to swim or do karate.

If you ever start thinking that your grandma doesn't look or act much like a grandma, that's just plain silly. God knew the kind of grandma you needed, and when she came along, He stretched the word "Grandma" to make it fit.

There's one more thing; some grandmas don't want to be called "grandma." Their grandchildren may call them "Nana," Yaya, "Granny," "Babi," or "Noni." It doesn't matter. Just like my grandma's hammock, the name you choose will fit, too, if she decides to change her mind –and grandmas often do.

CAN YOU HEAR ME NOW?

Giggles, shrieks, pattering feet,
Piano pieces, drumming,
Slamming door, steady roar,
Refrigerator humming,
Songs, tunes, silly cartoons
All form my favorite sound –
The sound that livens up these rooms
When grandkids are around.

#timetogohome
#soundofsilence
#mysecondfavoritesound

THE LAST TO LEAVE

The last of the family has gone.
Silence settles like sand in an hour glass.
Rooms that rang with laughter ring hollow.
Mugs and muffin crumbs clutter the counter.
Sheets wave goodbye from the clothesline outside,
And I feel as stripped as the beds they adorned last night.

TIMES AND SEASONS

Seasons remind us that life moves on

Whether or not we have a mind to.

ELEMENTAL ARTISTRY

Weather, paint upon your canvas
what you've wrought or soon will wreak.
Punctuate your storms with rainbows;
Form sundog parentheses.

Ebon clear but for the astral
Brush night skies before first frost;
And with strokes of clearest azure
Days when Bo-Peep clouds are lost.

Coat with red a morning's warning;
Scarlet orange an eve's delight.
Blend the prism's ordered palette
As the day accedes to night.

Gather dust from autumn's corn fields;
Fling into a sepia sky.
Then when winter trees are barren
Grayscale landscape clothe in white

Let March change her dirty dresses
Underneath a silvery moon;
April drench her gowns with luster,
Golden plait June's afternoon.

Elemental are your sketches
Varied in each hue and tone—
Awe creating, ever changing,
Never lacking, never done.

WILLOW SONGS

I don't know why I don't know how
The greening of the willow bough
Creates a longing in my breast
For springs long past.

The red winged black bird singing there
Could never know, could never care
That children hung on that same branch
And sang with mirth.

Those children now have older grown
And left the nest that was our home.
Who could predict, who would have guessed
They'd leave so soon?

Once muted tones of winter days
Designed my plans, defined my ways
Silence that fell like so much snow
Had dampened dreams.

But color burst; it has survived.
Yearnings thought dead have been revived
Melodious strains accompany
My heart's reply.

The greening of the willow bough
Gives essence to this life somehow;
Each season brings new songs, new life
And hearts expand.

THREE ROBUST ROBINS

Three robust robins reveled in this morning's warming sun.
They hopped about as Robins do, declaring Spring begun,
Excitedly discussing which strategies are best
For choosing the location of each families' feathered nest.

The strong and sturdy ash tree was found last year to be
The very place the cats chose as preferred residency
So, each fowl in turn examined its own potential perch…
Under deck, in lilac bush, or high up in the birch.

I watched them from my window as they met out on the lawn
A sign as sure as any that life on earth goes on.
My musings turned to Father God, Creator of all things
Who treasures things like robin nests as well as sparrow wings.

He tends, regards and nurtures every child and bird and beast
Granting worth and favor to those deemed as the least.
His heart is filled with pity for each fallen little bird.
How it must break when humans deem His promises absurd!

The robins quickly scattered when the cats went out to play
But I glimpsed their tireless striving as I labored through the day.
One poked under the clothesline, hoarding feathers, twigs and string
One strained against a worm, and one commenced to sing.

Bird ballads buoyed my spirit, and I joined in heavenly praise.
In this our God was honored on this earliest of spring days.
Approvingly God smiled upon the toils of hands and beaks
This homely worship won His heart…for praise is what He seeks.

CONTEMPLATING SPRING

I'm even with the treetops, soaking up the sun
Flittering yellow butterfly confirms spring has begun;

Entertained by angels making music in the leaves,
Earthy scent of pine swept up by Heaven's breeze.

Boastful crows caw loudly, finches trill in fun;
both gleefully proclaiming that winter's chill is done.

Dandelion heads poke up from dormant summer seeds;
Green grass complementing those defiant, playful weeds.

Communing with my Father through His Spirit and His Son
Inspiring life flows through me, breathing through all creation.

HAIL
(a haiku)

Ice like frozen fists
Pummel pound slice dice; dissolve
As dread from loss springs

SUMMER'S FIRST ROSE

Last week I spotted you,
Peeking from your hiding place.
Your face was pale, yet eager
For summer's warm embrace.

Yesterday you blushed
Where once no color graced your cheek.
Curiosity budded there;
Glistening, not so meek.

But oh, today you blossomed,
Boldly made your grand debut;
With confidence and valor,
Shouting "summer" in your hue.

And the summer gave you warmth
To radiate to those
Who look upon your lovely face
With admiration, Rose.

CLOTHESLINE CLEAN

She gives each pillowcase a snap;
Drapes the sheets across the line
And fastens them with wooden pins;
For wasting sunshine seems a sin
When summer breezes blow so fine,
Making bed sheets sway and flap.

From her kitchen now she sees
Linens curled; sheets unfurled
As if engaged in ritual,
Their antics light, ethereal
Waltzing garments whirl and twirl
Twixt greening grass and trees.

Soon bedding is collected,
Soft in arms outstretched
And hauled like treasure to the bed,
Sweet perfume filling her head
From bounteous load she's fetched
With scent of clean injected.

GARDEN ENCOUNTERS

I strolled barefoot to my garden.
Grass tickled between my toes.
Dewdrops sprinkled 'round my ankles.
Gnats buzzed boldly up my nose.

As I neared, the rhubarb rustled.
Purr-sy scampered into view.
Frightened robins all a-flutter
Chided loudly as they flew.

Near the lettuce, still and silent
Save her twitching nose and ear
Rabbit paused, then darted quickly
Guided wildly by her fear.

Running past, a squirrel took notice,
Then proceeded up a tree
Where he sat and scolded mildly,
Eyeing both my cat and me.

I began by cutting spinach.
Next, I felt for bulging peas.
Crunchy, sweet, a few sustained me
As I picked them on my knees.

From the pond a splashing clamor
Shook me from my reverie.
Drake was romancing his darling
Quacking, splattering noisily.

Soon their noise disturbed the gander
Guarding o'er his nesting goose.
Cantankerous, he honked a warning,
Flailing wings outstretched and loose.

Smiling, I returned to labor
Senses flooded, heart released,
And my praise began as humming.
As it grew, volume increased.

In the breeze cool and refreshing
Jesus whispered in my ear,
"I've been waiting all this morning.
I'm so glad you found me here."

(continued)

So, from there our chat proceeded
Up and down six rows of beans
As methodically I weeded
Through my worries, hopes and dreams.

Straightening, I surveyed with wonder
All my Father had bestowed.
Surprise! Atop my pile of produce
Perched a gray and wrinkled toad.

"Shoo," I said, and gently nudged him
'Till into the grass he hopped.
Quickly I picked up my treasures,
Although once again I stopped.

From beneath the tall potatoes
Something gave my foot a tap.
Mice-tro lazily stretched and pawed me,
Waking from his long cat-nap.

To the house I then retreated,
Cats frolicking in my way.
By my sweetheart I was greeted,
Quizzing me about my day.

Viewing me smudged and disheveled,
Sympathizing with his tone,
He remarked, "You worked for hours—
Too bad you had to work alone."

SCHOOL DAYS

Late August smells like chalk dust
Tastes like apples
Looks like imperfect lines of well-groomed children
Sounds like giggles
Feels dog tired by sundown.

ODE TO FALL

Crisp mornings in Fall
Are the nicest of all.
Frost shimmers and glows,
Steam flows from my nose.
The blue sky is clear
And the first sound I hear
Is the honking of geese
Disturbing my peace.
Leaves all a-flutter
Make colorful clutter
Across all the lawns
As daylight first dawns.
The landscape ignites
As the sun sheds its light.
It's warming up better
Though I still need a sweater.
Piles of pumpkins remind us
That summer's behind us.
Nippy nights Fall provides
For campfires and hayrides.
The full harvest moon
Will wane way too soon.
Oh, there's many a reason
Fall is my favorite season!

FOREVER FALL

When scarlet sumac fires raged,
Fine feathery fronds of pampas waved.
Midst pumpkins, squash and bittersweet,
You held my hands and vowed to be
My life's companion, ally, love;
The prince that I'd been dreaming of.
Cloudless evening's crimson warning
beckoned glistening frost by morning.

Three decades and a half have flown.
Love, through each season past, has grown.
Now fall's vibrant, leafy showers
Blanket summer's fading flowers.
Fair autumn scenes our senses fill.
Her breezes make us quiver still;
Lift rapturous hearts in whirling dance;
Stir memories and ignite romance.

NOW IT'S NOVEMBER

New month
New day
Change is in the air
Misty morning, nippy night
Call for outerwear
Jacket, sweater,
Vest of down
Umbrella at the ready
Fresh raked leaves,
Autumn fires
Have us feeling heady.

New order
New way
Gather, reap and stow.
Windows washed, chimney swabbed
Cobwebs have to go.
Potatoes, turkey,
Pumpkin pie
Soon will grace our table.
Family huddled
Will give thanks
And eat 'til we're not able.

DECEMBER DELIGHTS

Sounds crackly, jingly, exultant, silent
Looks snowy, shimmery, lit-up, ornate
Feels expectant, shivery, snuggly, joyful
Smells of pine, cinnamon, peppermint, spice
Tastes warm, sweet, rich, reminiscent
Brings traditions, faith, togetherness, love.

An
ever-
green
sprung from
tender sprout and
stretched its frail branches.
It grew
before the eyes
of men -just like a root
from dry, parched desert ground.
It was not beautiful, desirable, or majestic.
The tree was despised by men who coveted greatness.
It was a
malformed, rejected tree…
a blight…laughable, to say the least.
We were ashamed and hid our fickle faces
from the humble tree that offered more than it seemed to own.
We tried our best to fell it, to whittle it down to our size, to destroy it.
But the tree stood tall.
It extended its shade when the sun beat down.
It lent its strength when we needed something to lean on.
It provided shelter when vicious storms pounded and railed against us.
Strong limbs held every burden brought to the tree and hung on its branches.
Most importantly, the tree pointed the way to Heaven to those whose eyes would see.
In its prime the tree was brought down;
fractured and shattered, broken by the heavy weight of our
numerous burdens. Through no fault of its own, the tree had perished,
and with it, hope. For how could any good thing come from a dead, forsaken tree?
Many who witnessed its destruction sorrowfully turned their backs on the tree and wept;
They did not recognize this as God's perfect will. But life would return to the stricken tree,
and to those
whose burdens
rolled into the abyss
that dreadful, victorious day.
Joy to the world, the Lord is come!
EVERGREEN: ISAIAH 53

FOR JUST ONE DAY

For just one day
we will not go
into the city
or the town.
I'm thinking, though,
we'll light a fire
to sit around
with those we know
and love who will be home
...for just one day.

For just one day
we'll tolerate
unbridled joy,
excessive noise,
squeals from children
gleefully
unwrapping toys
with laser sounds
and high-pitched squawks
...for just one day.

For just one day
we'll disregard
high calories
and extra fat,
plus sugared things
we ought to shun.
Tomorrow we'll go back to that,
but we'll have candy,
pie, and fudge
...for just one day.

For just one day
we'll set aside
our differences,
our selfish pride.
We'll do our best
to keep the peace
and not take sides.
We know we must
because it's right
...for just one day.

(continued)

For just one day
we'll light the wicks
of candles we
have never lit;
use fine china,
crystal too;
in merriment
wipe dust from games
we rarely play
...for just one day.

For just one day
the world will slow—
perhaps not kneel,
but genuflect;
pay homage to
our God and King,
show some respect.
This side of Heaven
it's what we get
...for just one day.

LIGHTS OF CHRISTMAS

PAST

- Lamps illumine dusty streets, lighting weary travelers' paths.
- Stars wink knowingly overhead, reflecting their Creator's radiance. He who knows their names, will soon bridge heaven and earth.
- Glaringly conspicuous, one star outshines the rest: delighting the dreamer, captivating the curious, luring the wise.
- Faltering lamps are soon put out as darkness descends and destinations are reached.
- Lustrous moon outlines landscape, edging it in sliver. Long shadows wearily stretch in its glow, resting while they can.
- Flickering candle's beam lights a barn and the Savior's way into the world.
- Hope and love shimmer through strained, tired eyes.
- Wet with water and blood, trembling infant glistens 'neath moon and candle's gleam.
- Twinkling stars reflect in donkey's brass and cow's bell.
- Astonishing, indescribable radiance…the glory of the Lord…overwhelms awestruck shepherds.

PRESENT

- Brightly colored bulbs frame twinkling trees in picture perfect windows.
- Brilliant white lights sparkle, dressing shrubs, fences, and otherwise naked tree limbs.
- Sheen of glass is brightened by candle's gleam in each polished palatial pane.
- Glowing candy canes form lines to Santa Claus.
- Glaring signs flash storefront boasts and bargains.
- Glitz and glitter adorn holiday revelers.
- Glint of gold and crystal adorn lavishly laden tables.
- Luminous neighborhoods attract, compete: most lights, most festive, most extravagant, most tasteful, most…
- Inflated, illumined snowmen, penguins, and snow globes stand as tall as the houses behind them -fake, iridescent snowflakes fluttering inside.
- Vivid choreographed displays of carefully positioned bulbs set to rhythmic seasonal tunes flash, blink, and dance across sculpted lawns.
- Lights in rapturous hearts set on hills throughout the world shimmer in remembrance and anticipation.

FUTURE

- In blazing glory the Light of the world returns astride lustrous white horse.
- No further need or desire for light exists.

COMFORT AND JOY
(Interspersed with lines from *"God Rest Ye Merry Gentlemen."*)

You know my human tendency to worry and to fret.
God rest ye, merry gentlemen, let nothing you dismay
You told me just to trust in you, yet often I forget.
Remember Christ, the Savior was born on Christmas Day
So, you sent a Comforter— a presence I can feel—
To save us all from Satan's power when we were gone astray
To wrap yourself around me and convince me that you're real.

    O tidings of comfort and joy, comfort and joy
The more I lose myself in you, the more stress melts away,
    O tidings of comfort and joy
With comfort adequate for each concern of every day.

Then from that comfort grows a fruit my heart can now employ;
Now to the Lord sing praises all you within this place
A deep exhilarating force comes bubbling out as joy!
And with true love and brotherhood each other now embrace
I take it with me as I work and play and rest and plan.
This holytide of Christmas doth bring redeeming grace
I share it just as much and just as often as I can.

    O Tidings of comfort and joy, comfort and joy
It isn't bound by circumstance or lessened by a trial
    O tidings of comfort and joy
Your comfort fills my heart and the proof is in my smile.

TWO YEARS CONVERGED

Two years converged at midnight's stroke:
One behind, and one before;
One spent, and one as yet unsullied;
One known, and one a mystery to be unraveled;
One polished (however imperfectly), and
One plump with possibilities.

NEW YEAR'S EVE

Here we meet, as always, bidding one more year farewell.
The guest list hasn't changed in fifteen years.
The setting is familiar and the faces are the same.
Savory treats await us, and John's new Christmas game.
Much gaiety and laughter fill the house as midnight nears.
The fire crackles cheerily as conversations swell.

Nothing much has changed, or so you might believe.
We gather, wearing boas, hats and bling.
Anticipation grows as the clock is counted down.
Loud honks and bells ring out, then kisses all around.
Someone starts out low, and soon everybody sings,
"Should auld acquaintance be forgot?" not *this* New Year's Eve!

Now our voices soften, and we look into each face.
Highlights and memories shared are brought to mind.
The year has changed and molded us in ways we hadn't thought.
We reminisce and ponder, offer comfort where it's sought.
To what this new year holds our eyes are blind,
And yet with joy we greet it --its challenges embrace.

Well past the midnight hour the revelry has ceased,
And with it goes the last of our denial.
We are now the old folks...Our parents, mostly dead.
Our children left at nine to put *their* kids to bed.
The thought could make us cringe, but instead it makes us smile.
God gave us friends so with each year our joy would be increased

BACK TO THE FUTURE
(a sevenling)

Look back for insight
Glean from experience
Wisdom inspired light

Look forward for hope
Opportunity thrives
When viewed through widened scope

Let go your past to find your future

UNINVITED

Uninvited, Winter seeps
Through crevices and cracks
Creeping in like chills
Crawling up our backs.
Icy fingers spread,
Gripping grass and tree;
Strangling, life extracting digits
Threaten by degree.
Fragile blooms succumb
And wither to the ground
As naked limbs scrape the skies
For mercy to be found.
Choking, ghastly clouds cough
Frigid sleet and snow,
And fling them far and wide
through wintry winds that blow.
All is held in winter's grasp—
Hampered, stopped, or slowed.
Barren lies the soil
Where seeds and bulbs were sown.
Unseen beneath the dirt, the ice, and snow,
Hope lies serene,
Confident of awakening to
The gentle kiss of spring.

PERSPECTIVE

How seldom does a cloud bring sweet relief--
No dark, disturbing, pounding gales of grief.
Shade and refresh me from the searing sun,
Renew me for the race that I must run.

How seldom does the sun embrace my soul--
No blazing, burning wielding of control.
Warm and tender breath upon my brow,
Permeate my being even now.

How seldom does the wind stir thoughts of love--
No thunderous, thrashing tempests from above.
Welcome breezes whisper round my head,
Whisk away the hurt and pain I dread.

How seldom does the rain dissolve my fears--
No flooding, flushing, mixing with my tears.
Gentle mist so cool against my skin,
Cleanse my heart and make me smile again.

How seldom does the snow drift lightly down--
No stinging, searing sleet to make me frown.
Delicate, dainty flakes melt on my face,
Remind me of God's pure and perfect grace.

FOR THE YOUNG

And all who regard frogs as future princes…

SWISH, HUSH, SHUSH-A-BYE

Daddy, what's that chirping sound that's coming from the hall?
A cricket calling for its love, my darling. That is all.
But Daddy, what's the loud "harrumph" from way down by the pond?
Frogs are singing lullabies to tadpoles that have spawned.
The mama duck is quacking. Why isn't she asleep?
From hungry owls and foxes her ducklings she must keep.

Swish, hush, shush-a-bye, rustle, hustle who
wings, sings, brushes by whispering, "God loves you."

I think I hear a siren. Don't policemen go to bed?
They work all through the nighttime to keep us safe, instead.
Do other people work at night? O Daddy tell me, please.
Doctors, nurses, firemen are just a few of these.
If just a few, then won't you tell me, Daddy, are there more?
Hush, my child, and I will tell of night workers galore:

Swish, hush, shush-a-bye, rustle, hustle who
wings, sings, brushes by whispering, "God loves you."

Workers stocking grocery shelves and people sorting mail,
Pilots, cabbies, bus drivers, and those who guard the jail,
Bakers making doughnuts, birthday cakes, and treats;
Semi drivers transporting groceries, milk, and meat;
People printing newspapers, others selling gas,
Construction workers mending roads so travelers can pass...

Swish, hush, shush-a-bye, rustle, hustle who
wings, sings, brushes by whispering, "God loves you."

Listen now, my precious child, before you close your eyes.
Another One is wide awake. He's loving, strong, and wise.
Those other workers go to sleep while you are wide awake.
But He is always on the job, a guardian for your sake.
He is the great Almighty God. You are His treasure rare.
So do not worry, little one, you're always in His care.

Swish, hush, shush-a-bye, rustle, hustle who
wings, sings, brushes by whispering, "God loves you."

OF WINGS AND THINGS

Upon a strand of gossamer there hung a fairy's wing.
It spun and sparkled in the sun, the daintiest of things.
A human touch would wither it as sure as June bugs whine,
Or feline foot demolish its most intricate design.

Just how the wing became unhinged is anybody's guess.
What remedy exists for such an empyrean mess?
A sprinkle of bee pollen and a dash of fairy dust
Applied by skilled and spritely gnome who's gained the fairies' trust.

The fairy's wing will be restored by morning's faintest light
For gnomes and fairies, as we know, both work and play by night.

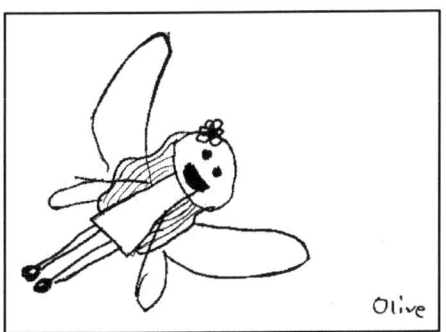

UMBRELLAS

Red, green, yellow, and blue,
Striped, plaid, and polka-dot, too—

Bobbing up, bobbing down,
The umbrella parade has come to town.

People coming, people going,
Umbrella tops with raindrops glowing.

Pitter-patter, friendly chatter,
The rain coming down doesn't matter.

Splashes, dashes, thunder crashes—
These are times of umbrella flashes.

THE TALE OF HALEY HALL

Outside a certain city near a pleasant neighborhood
Stood a tall, inviting forest that the children called "The Wood."
No one knows quite how it started, but nearly every day
The children packed their lunches, then entered "The Wood" to play.

Yes, all the children went to play, that is, except for two.
"You're little," sneered the others, "There's not much that you can do."
As the kids set out each morning to run and romp and hunt,
They rudely snubbed poor Haley Hall as well as Felix Funt.

"Be sure you're home for dinner, son," instructed Mrs. Hall,
"And today you're taking Haley. She's your sister, after all."
"Aw, Mom!" the boy protested, but his mother's narrowed eyes
Soon had her son persuaded. Haley whooped at the surprise.

The children quickly gathered just beyond the garden wall.
Accusingly they grumbled, "you brought Haley Hall the Small?!"
"I had to," groaned her brother as Haley plugged her ears.
She donned her pink sunglasses to hide her brimming tears.

Haley joined the group despite the insults that were hurled.
Their protests became milder as she strolled into their world.
The path was cool and shady, though at times the sun broke through.
Haley thought she was in Heaven. It seemed too good to be true.

The joy Haley was feeling came abruptly to an end.
A large rope net descended as they curved around the bend.
"Stop right there!" A voice demanded, "for now you have to pay."
"Drop your lunches in the basket and you'll soon be on your way."

"Who are you?" Haley's brother begged, his voice quaking with fear.
"I'm Thomas Tate the Great," it boomed. "Obey me! Do you hear?"
So one by one, begrudgingly, they let their lunches fall.
The last to reach the basket was Haley Hall the Small.

Haley's stomach rumbled as she knelt to tie her shoe.
With a brief but fervent prayer she asked God what she should do.
Rare courage swelled within her and her eyes lit up with hope.
Then she stood and started scaling the net made out of rope.

"Go back! Get down, I tell you!" Thomas roared from the treetop.
But nothing he could do or say could make brave Haley stop.
The children stared in wonder, still frozen where they stood,
Wishing they had never left their pleasant neighborhood.

(continued)

Haley kept on climbing 'til she disappeared from sight.
A rustling of the branches made the children scream with fright.
An object came a-tumbling and crashing to the ground.
With caution they approached; a megaphone is what they found.

From above came a commotion, then Haley's voice exclaimed,
"You aren't Thomas Tate the Great… and *you* should be ashamed!"
"It's okay," Haley hollered. "We have nothing more to fear.
It's only Felix Funt!" "…THE RUNT?" the children jeered.

Haley and a sheepish Felix Funt climbed down at last.
As the group rushed forth in anger Haley interceded fast.
"No harm was done," she told them. "Felix hasn't spoiled our plan."
"I was wrong," Felix admitted. "Please forgive me if you can."

Some voiced their disapproval, and some just scratched their head.
Then Haley's brother cleared his throat and this is what he said,
"Felix Funt and sister Haley, we've been selfish and unkind.
You both have lots of courage. Our pride has made us blind."

"We underrated both of you, based only on your size.
We teased you and we taunted, now our sins we realize.
Haley, we commission you as queen of all 'The Wood.'
Felix, you'll defend her. Use your cleverness for good."

"We are now your loyal subjects, and it's just as Jesus said.
Those who want to be the first will be the last instead;
while those who are the least will be the greatest of them all."
That's how our heroine became Queen Haley Hall the Small.

HOLD THAT PENCIL

Look at the things you brought to school,
your crayons, scissors, glue.
Among your new supplies
you'll find a pencil, too.

Today we'll learn to hold this tool-
Maybe you know how.
Try it 'til you get it right,
then take a little bow.

Your thumb and pointer finger
Should grip your pencil tight.
Pinch it just above the lead
When you prepare to write.

Your tall man curls up underneath
Offering his side
So pencil has a place to rest
While going for a ride.

The last two fingers also curl,
hidden from your view.
I'd like to see you try it-
It's not so hard to do.

Keep practicing; you'll catch on soon.
It's easy as can be.
We'll start by writing letters
Like A and B and C.

Once you've learned your letters you can
Form them into words.
And words make poems and stories
As you, no doubt, have heard.

And stories take us anywhere
We've ever dreamed to go.
They tell our thoughts and feelings,
Help imaginations grow.

Pencils aren't just useful tools;
They soon will be your friends.
May your love for writing
Start today and never end.

CHILLS

The night was dark and all was still.
I stumbled up the rocky hill.

The moon was shining full and free,
Staring from the sky at me.

Suddenly two eyes appeared.
They looked so wide and round and weird.

I tripped and fell right to the ground.
The night was still –there was no sound.

The eyes came close. I just lay still;
And down my back I felt a chill.

Then through the night there shrieked a sound…
Whoo – whoo –it sounded all around.

It came from where the two eyes were;
An owl! At last I made a stir.

I stood up straight, then ran on home
And quickly penned this chilling poem.

ARRIVAL AND SURVIVAL OF THE CITY KIDS

The cousins all came to visit last week.
They arrived in their city clothes, stylish and sleek.
Uncle told Daddy, voice edged with alarm,
"My kids need to spend some time on the farm.
They're lazy and soft and don't have a clue.
I'm sure you and Marge will know just what to do."

Like Daddy and Ma don't have enough to do without babysitting.

Each left the mini-van wiping their tears,
Backpacks in hand, wires hung from their ears;
Zach with his I-pod, Rochelle's DVD,
Jed's portable lap-top, a Game Boy for Leigh.
The first thing Dad did was collect each device
And hide them away. He didn't blink twice.

Do they think they're on vacation or something?

Ma called us to dinner. She'd made quite a spread:
Sliced parsnips, fresh peas, and homemade rye bread,
Lamb burgers, taters, and strawberry pie.
They turned up their noses and passed it on by.
Daddy observed them, arching his brow.
Such finicky eating he'd never allow.

I can't wait to see what happens tomorrow after Uncle leaves!

The boys did the dishes, the girls made the beds;
Two rows 'cross the floor, with heads matching heads.
Then, in the dark, we cousins -all seven-
Whispered and giggled 'til way past eleven.
"Hush! Don't you know you'll be up before long?"
Dad hollered, "the farm chores begin before dawn."

I'll bet they think he's foolin'.

Of course, Daddy woke us at quarter to five.
How would those city kids ever survive?
Jed helped milk the cows and Rochelle slopped the hogs.
We gathered the eggs, then fed cats and dogs,
Gave corn to the chickens, and fed lambs their bottles,
Then Zach mowed the hay field with tractor full-throttle.

If I didn't know better, I'd think he was having fun.

(continued)

We rode the hay wagon and baled up the hay,

Then up in the loft we stacked it away.
When dinner time came and the platters were passed
Each morsel was eaten, right down to the last;
Then straight to our beds with nary a whimper,
And all without Daddy once losing his temper.

Like Daddy would dust THEIR britches, anyway.

After that first day, we mixed work with fun.
We swam in the horse tank and dried in the sun,
Played tag after dark –the whole cousin clan-
And swung in the hayloft on ropes like Tarzan;
Then back in the corner Leigh glimpsed a cat's paw
And discovered new kittens curled up in the straw.

You would-a thought she found gold or something.

Our cousins left Sunday; that day was our last.
We cried as we hugged them; the week went too fast.
We gave them zucchini, tomatoes, and beets,
Carrots and corn and a kitten named "Deetz."
They aren't city kids now, as this story ends;
Turns out our four cousins are really our friends.

Hey, wait! They forgot their stuff...
I-pod, DVD player, laptop and Game Boy. (GRIN)
They'll be back soon.

A BUNNY AND PIG TALE

Bianca bunny bounced
Upon her trampoline
Wishing for a friend to
Join in her brisk routine.

Who should come upon her
But plump Peony Pig
Who couldn't jump one inch
Or even dance a jig.

So forlorn was she that
Bianca made a plan –
"Peony, you will jump.
I am convinced you can."

First, she made a ramp that
Peony could walk up.
Then she started jumping,
Refusing to let up.

Peony's eyes were wide
When finally, she bounced.
She giggled and she squealed;
Her great success announced.

Bianca gave her all.
Peony bounced so high
She thought that she would sail
Away into the sky.

They took each other's hands,
Held on with all their might
And even higher flew
Like feathers airy, light

Peony tumbled down,
Rolled up against her friend;
They laughed and made a wish that
The day would never end.

The moral to this tale
When all is said and done?
Double up your efforts;
Two is better than one.

COOKIES
(a synonym diamante)

Cookies
Scrumptious confections
Crumble, crunch, munch
Cordial comforts, savory sentiments
sweets

HIDE AND SQUEAK
(a verb poem)

Peek squeak streak
Tremble nimble quiver quake
Spy eye sigh

Growl prowl pounce
Batter buffet pummel munch
Slurp burp purr

LOOSE LIPS SINK SHIPS

She knows everything and tells all she knows.
Gossip is shared before it gets old;
And nothing is
Off limits, too risky, or too hurtful.
Loose lips sink ships –
And that includes friendships.

ANGER'S PATH

I often do things I regret
when I am cranky, fuming, mad.
I grumble, mumble, quarrel, fret;
it makes my Father very sad.

While feeling sorry for myself,
Anger looms, matches my stride
convincing me -that impish elf-
of rights denied and injured pride.

I pay him precious little heed,
and yet I do not bid him, "Go."
So like a tiny thistle seed
that fiendish elf begins to grow.

Soon Anger stretches into Grudge.
That brute, I fear, is here to stay.
I shout, "Be gone!" He does not budge,
no matter what I do or say.

Grudge won't be satisfied it seems,
unless I seek his mate, Revenge.
Invading consciousness and dreams
he steers me on a spiteful binge.

Although it seems a just reward
Revenge will never say, "Enough."
No longer do I seek accord;
my tender heart turns cold and tough.

The path I've hiked with Anger led
to heartache, agony and pain.
His reappearance makes me dread
to keep his company again.

Yet God says Anger is okay
if I am careful not to sin;
relinquish it, forgive, and pray
before I go to sleep again.

In your anger do not sin:
Do not let the sun go down while you are still angry.
(Ephesians 4:26 New International Version Bible)

LEGEND OF A BUSH AND A TREE

A bush sprang up in the middle of the desert.
It muddled in a puddle in the pouring rain.
When the puddle dried up the bush fried up
'Cuz the roots couldn't creep through the sand so deep.

Oh, the sun beat down and it cracked the ground
And the roots didn't find any water around.
The green leaves withered and the worms they slithered
Into the rotten wood that wasn't any good.

A tree grew up nearby the living water
let its roots shoot down 'til they found the stream.
Its green buds popped, and they never ever stopped.
When the weather grew dry its branches didn't fry.

Oh, the sun beat down and it cracked the ground
But the roots were long, and the tree grew strong.
The leaves stayed as green as any you have seen
And the tree bore fruit and a brand-new shoot.

Now the bush in the desert is a man that is foolish.
He learns, and he yearns for the ways of man.
But his crimes are bold and his heart grows cold.
He can only blame his sin for the pickle he is in.

Oh, the sun beats down and it cracks the ground
But his roots can't find any water around.
So, his life it withers and the serpent slithers
o'er his heart of stone that is sad and all alone.

The tree by the water is a man full of wisdom.
He learns, and he yearns for the ways of God.
And God makes him new as only He can do.
He is fruitful and free and as happy as can be.

Oh, the sun beats down and it cracks the ground
But his roots are long, and his faith is strong.
So, he won't fret about a storm or a drought
And God receives the glory for his amazing story.

(Based on Jeremiah 17)

A LITTLE MORE

Some folks say, "Wherever you go
Leave things as they were before."
I concur, but add this to it:
Do that and a little more.
Ask yourself as you are leaving
If the place where you have been
Benefited by your presence.
Is it better now than then?

Have you been a ray of sunshine?
Offered humor or a prayer?
Found a way to serve the server?
Shown how much you really care?
As you leave just ask these questions:
Did I listen more than speak?
Were my actions gifts of kindness?
Whose approval did I seek?

Some folks say, "A job is done when
Expectations have been met."
I would say that once you meet them
You are not quite finished yet.
Do a little something extra
Even if you've done your share.
It's the cherry on the sundae;
It's the ribbon in the hair.

Don't be satisfied with so-so;
You are gifted, you are blessed.
Just as long as you are able
Offer up your very best.
You won't always be rewarded;
Some will fail to understand.
But your self-respect will blossom,
Opportunities expand.

WHIMSY
...a product of playful or capricious fancy

...To make you think,

Or smile,

Or scratch your head...

BEGINNER'S ANGST

Beginning is the thing
That gets in the way
Of accomplishing much;
Because, of course, a thing
To be done must first be begun.
And beginning a thing requires
Thinking, goal setting,
Strategic planning –if you want
The thing to succeed, that is;
And why begin something
Doomed not to succeed?
Risk and re-prioritizing –both are
Required for good beginnings.
"Finish well!" they say.
But before you finish
(Let alone finish well),
You must begin. And therein
Lies the problem.

YOUR SMILE

Your smile is a crocus on a snowy March day,
The scent of lilacs early in May,
A happy surprise as I go on my way, your smile.

Your smile is a breeze sent to mellow the sun,
The taste of water when the race is run,
A cool comfort sought that is second to none, your smile.

Your smile is a handwritten letter you send,
A sight for sore eyes from the hand of a friend,
A sweet sentiment thoughtfully penned, your smile.

Your smile is a melody played high and clear,
The sound of the birds chirping with cheer,
A familiar, harmonious song in my ear, your smile.

Your smile is something I've come to count on,
Like the feel of bare feet on a newly mown lawn,
A fond memory even after you've gone, your smile.

TO ASK OR NOT TO ASK

The question dangles
between them-
warm, sticky air
holding it there
unnoticed, ignorable
to all but the asker
who isn't asking
except in her head.

Possible scenes play out,
eager to free
the hovering question
wrangling, strangling
conversation
while the asker
who isn't asking
silently poses it a dozen ways.

She wants an answer;
Or dose she?
Shivering despite
sweltering heat,
courage wanes
doubts rise
and she walks away,
question suspended there still.

HOW I GET AROUND

My Odyssey hums –vroom, vroom
And faithfully runs –zoom, zoom
No put-a-put-put or rut-a-tut-tut
She hums and whistles and sings.

She whisks me around –vroom, vroom
All over the town –zoom, zoom
With nary a fear she zips me back here
When I am done for the day.

RUMMAGING AND REMINISCING

Mismatched silverware $10
Hey, this spoon is the pattern I had growing up.
Depression glass bowl $20
This matches Grandma's dishes in the china cupboard!
The Poky Little Puppy book (slightly dog-eared) $3
I loved that story as a little girl!
Daisy Dukes $5 each
What're Daisy Dukes? You don't need to know.
Antique utility cart $15
Your great-great grandma's toaster sat on one of those.
Tupperware popsicle set $4
I think I still have mine! Let's make popsicles.
Dotted Swiss curtains $8
My graduation dress was dotted swiss!
LP Albums $5 each
Those are record albums, Sweetie, not giant CD's.
Garage sales
Where junk comes at a price but memories are free

SO I'VE BEEN THINKING…
(a monotetra)

"So I've been thinking dear," she said –
The statement seized his heart with dread;
Ideas small were bound to spread.
What lay ahead? What lay ahead?

We need to change this room's décor.
For starters we'll tear out the floor
Install a new sliding barn door
And there is more; and there is more.

That old light fixture we'll replace;
Knock out this wall to add some space;
Add accent wall and fireplace
With a stone face; with a stone face.

He knew it useless to protest,
So, to her plans he acquiesced.
He'd soon re-feathered their whole nest.
She was impressed. She was impressed.

"So I've been thinking dear," said he
It's time we did without TV
HGTV especially.
Can we agree? Can we agree?

REVELATION

The face I daily scrub, pluck,
Moisturize, conceal,
Smooth, bronze, and
Highlight is familiar;
Pleasant even.
Why then am I shocked
By the face peering
From this photo-
So unlike
The one that grins
From my mirror
Of a morning?
This face is pale, splotchy,
Lined, wrinkled, old...
Much like I remember
My grandmother's.

THE PROBLEM WITH STARTING A DIET

The problem with starting a diet
is finding the gumption to try it,
for chocolate and pasta entices
much more so than celery slices.

While watching a friend slurp a milkshake,
who wants to nibble a rice cake?
Or sip on tea from Ceylon
Before all the brownies are gone?

The problem with starting a diet
Is willpower— I cannot deny it.
My compulsion to eat junk is valid.
Is Chex mix considered a salad?

TO DO OR NOT TO DO

I need to clean the kitchen
And mop the bathroom floors
The garden should be weeded
There's tons of work outdoors

My photos all need sorting
The rugs should all be shook
I have to bathe the kitty
It's time I write my book

The laundry bag is bulging
My lesson plans aren't made
I haven't cleared my inbox
The bills have not been paid

This list, it wants to own me
But it won't have its way
Beside the words *TO DO*
I'm writing *NOT TODAY*

SELF MOTIVATION

You might wonder, with so much to do,
Why I take time for the daily Sudoku.
Perhaps you think it improves math skills
Makes me sharp, multiplies brain cells;
Or maybe you consider it puzzle therapy,
A way to unwind- un-grump my grumpy.
But here I shall most humbly confess
The real motivation is much, much less.
I do Sudoku simply so I can say,
"Look here! I finished something today."

THE LAST DONUT

The last donut is the least favorite.
But it's still a donut. So, because it's last
It becomes the most desired donut of all.
But nobody admits they want it,
So each takes a turn circling the box
Eyeing that donut —nonchalantly of course.
Some make gestures feigning disgust;
Others stop to pick up bits of glaze or a nut.
The charade continues for minutes, hours
Until that moment when nobody is
Watching the box —almost nobody, that is.
And suddenly the last donut is gone.
And everyone looks for a telltale crumb
On someone's chin. But someone is trying
Not to let on that they, in one swift movement,
Snarfed down the last donut —because someone had to.
You're welcome.

SHOPPING EXPERT, FABULOUS FRIEND

Her husband is a softball star;
one son plays basketball.
Baseball is the others' game;
her girl loves volleyball.
My friend is not an athlete
but she outlasts them all
in the venue of her choosing—
the local shopping mall.

A funny, smart, and perky gal,
she wears size six petite,
tracking sales and fashion trends,
cute sneakers on her feet.
She sifts through bargain tables
unwilling to retreat
'til she proclaims her victory,
waving a sales receipt.

She's thrifty and she's practical,
savvy about textiles.
Scouring fashion magazines
she learns the latest styles.
She's memorized store layouts,
arrangement of the aisles,
and routes to stores and outlet malls
within three hundred miles.

Her shopping is methodical,
not careless or slipshod.
Those who dare accompany her
observe amazed and awed.
Shoppers half her age give up,
exhausted and slack-jawed;
her stamina and strategy
they reverently applaud.

I've been under her tutelage
For twenty-something years—
shopped for nearly everything
from soup to black brassieres.
Managers know her by name,
and so do most cashiers.
I have seen her wit and prowess
reduce grown men to tears.

(continued)

Don't think her superficial,
her profundity I'll plead;
kind-hearted, loving, faithful
and virtuous indeed.
She isn't moved by money
or galvanized by greed.
She'd give the Ricci off her back
to help someone in need.

Sometimes we plan a shopping day,
sometimes a whole weekend,
I seek her sound advisement;
ask what she'd recommend.
On her candid opinions
I cheerfully depend.
No person knows me better than
my boutique loving friend.

The bonding that has taken place
as we've trekked sale to sale
could only have occurred on
the turf they call "retail."
It underlies our zest and
attention to detail.
No doubt it's aided by the fact
that we are both female.

Through happy times and difficult
we've watched our friendship bloom.
We've shared our deepest secrets,
and food we can't consume.
We've swapped our kids and coupons
and tried on French perfume.
We've laughed so hard we had to run
to find the Ladies' room.

Frugality describes my friend;
she's also very smart.
She has refined her hobby
to something of an art.
Only things of quality
are placed into her cart.
I'm honored that she found a place
for me within her heart.

JADED

Tell me the things you want me to know
Like the things you do and the places you go,
What makes you happy, angry or sad,
How you redeem a day that is bad.
Tell me your plans, your hopes, and your dreams,
And soon I will know if it's all as it seems.
Be all that you say, authentic and true.
When what's said is done is when I'll believe you

I MIGHT BE CRAZY
(a reverse poem – please read in its entirety)

I might be crazy
But I refuse to believe
Our president is heartless
I know you may not agree that
He is an honest, brilliant leader
Lies abound, some even claiming that
Our president is immoral and narcissistic
I wholeheartedly concur that
Securing America's borders
Is more important than
Showing compassion to non-Americans
But I tell you this
We, the people, make America great!
To protect our liberties
We need to build a border wall
Though some believe
The cost of building a wall is excessive
I do attest
A wall is our greatest need
It is foolish to believe that
Truth and righteousness will prevail
If our nation's borders aren't secure
Still I profess
I am first and foremost a Christian

Now read this from the bottom up

FOOLS

Each one of us is a fool, I'd say
At least in some particular way:
A fool for love, a fool for a cause,
For God, for country, or just because.

Sometimes we know but pretend we do not.
We cling to the foolish with all that we've got.
Then watch as it crumbles, dissolves or fades
Making us rue the choices we've made.

But once in a while the foolish proves wise
And this, despisers of fools despise-
That what was deemed foolish was not as it seemed
And the fool becomes, in the end, esteemed.

And those who live by their self-made rules
While despising God are actually fools;
While the fools according to this world's lies
Are chosen by God to confuse the wise.

A VISITOR'S CANADIAN ANTHEM

O Canada! Your highways stretch for miles.
They're threatening our over-eager smiles.
We fear the road shall never end;
but just when we are sure,
our guide begins the tour.

O Canada! Across your prairies wide
I feel a rhythmic rocking side to side
as grasses wave and breezes blow.
I'm feeling mighty sick.
Oh Dramamine, come quick!

O Canada! Your cities buzz with life—
museums, shopping, restaurants, nightlife—
best seen in summertime, of course.
Your fashion, culture, art
are modern, hip, and smart.

O Canada! Your famous people shine.
Kurt Browning and Wayne Gretzky skate so fine.
Shania, Keanu, Celine
are but a dazzling few
who tip their hats to you.

O Canada! Your wilderness is wild,
and there I feel as if I've been exiled;
cumbersome pack upon my back
while path grows winding, steep
for miles before I sleep.

O Canada! I've glimpsed your creatures fierce:
brown bears and loons whose cries my eardrums pierce,
your fearsome goose and mighty moose.
Mosquitoes large as crows
eat me right through my clothes.

O Canada! Your rivers and your streams
run clearer than the visions in my dreams.
I pray before I take a drink
that parasites are dead
and there no moose have tread.

O Canada! O Canada!
O Canada! I still am glad I came.
O Canada! I love you all the same.

FISHIN' FOR MEN

"Ernie, put yer waders on.
Go grab yer pole an' lure.
Reckon I don't hafta tell
ya' what them things are fer.

Now tell th' missus s'long
then hop in this here truck.
Down yon at Lake Kahoochee
we'll try our trollin' luck.

I sure 'nuf knows it's Sunday,
but 'tisn't ever' day
th' catfish are a bitin'
same as they are t'day.

Besides, it's by the churchyard.
We'll hear th' choir singin'.
We'll have a taste o' Heaven
while our catch we're stringin'.

I musta been convincin';
'took less than a minute.
Th' missus ain't too happy?
Shoot! She'll soon forget it.

Now Hold th' worm can, Ernie.
--dug 'em fresh this mornin'.
I ain't got time fer preachin';
it's oh so dry, an' borin'.

Reckon th' times a'comin'
I'll hafta change my ways.
'Til then I'll jes' keep fishin'.
Ain't got no need t' pray.

Yer mighty quiet, Ernie.
Th' cat done got yer tongue?
Now you'll forget th' missus
Soon as yer line is flung.

That's Blindman's Knob we're climbin'
--nearly there, by jiggered!
We both can get t' baitin'
quicker than I figgered.

(continued)

Doggone it! Nothin's happnin'...
I'm pushin' on th' brake!
Good Lawd! We are a headin'
straight for Kahoochee Lake!"

Now Deacon Joe wuz fixin'
fer Sunday's meetin' when
he heard a loud commotion
an' shoutin', cursin' men.

He scurried through the meadow
an' down the slipp'ry bank
in time t' see Lyle's pick-up
jes' sinkin' like a tank.

The two men thrashed an' hollered
t' save their drownin' souls.
Out there among the rushes
Joe found their fishin' poles.

Joe cast an' hooked Lyle's britches
an' as he reeled him in,
Lyle snagged Ernie's suspenders;
he stretched 'em mighty thin!

Two wet an' red-faced anglers
flopped on Kahoochee's shore.
They thanked the Lord in Heaven
t' be on land once more.

"Well fellas, I'll be headin'
back over t' th' church.
Guess you'll be comin' with me
since yer left in th' lurch."

Joe hooked one arm through Ernie's,
th' other one through Lyle's.
folks saw that passel comin'
An' they broke into smiles.

Down front, right near th' altar
Ernie caught his missus.
A worm crawled down her cheek as
he laid on the kisses.

(continued)

A humbled Lyle and Ernie
both took to repentin'.
Th' preacher let 'em finish
then did his commentin'.

"This here's an illustration
of a truth y'all have heard.
Ol' Deacon Joe is righteous
an' listens t' God's Word.

'An when he sees a sinner
a-drownin' in his ways
old Joe'll go a fishin'
th' dyin' soul t' save.

Some folks don't meet th' Savior
While sittin' in a pew.
They hafta git reminded
a' what God's grace can do.

So boys, keep up yer fishin'.
But ever' now an' then,
instead o' snaggin' catfish
go fishin' fer some men."

"The fruit of the uncompromisingly righteous is a tree of life, and he who is wise captures human lives for God, as a fisher of men--he gathers and receives them for eternity."
(Proverbs 11:30 Amplified Bible)

TOO MUCH INFORMATION

You tell me things that I
Would rather not know.
Not now. Not ever. However,
Now those things weigh on me
Like a pail of water hauled
From Grandpa's well.
I weigh your
Facts against mine,
Ponder innuendos,
Parse insinuations.
And observe. Mostly observe.

RESOLVE

"It's just a sweet little kitten," she said.
"How much trouble can she cause?"
And as he looked into those eyes
(Whose eyes, I can't be sure),
His resolve melted into a saucer of cream that
Kitten licks from her whiskers each morning
While sitting on his keyboard.

THE STRAY

Hiss!
I rush to discover
what agitates
poor Kitty so.
Through frost-flecked window
I glimpse
matted fur-ball
peering in,
fire dancing in opalescent eyes—
our fire—
dispelling the cold,
drawing him.

Flick!
Porch light
shimmers, illumines;
he whirls,
disappearing in a flash,
leaving behind
a tuft of fur
and a pound of
pity.
He knows
he doesn't
belong here.

THREE HAIKUS

GRANDGIRLS

Utter poetry
Delightful lyrical belles
Sweet grandgirls of mine

LET'S WALTZ

Smooth steps; three-four time
Left right close back together
Whisk weave rise and fall

MIXED EMOTIONS

Shining like silver
Raindrop gems glisten on glass
Too merry too pert

COMPLEX
(an acrostic)

C arry on-
n**O**thing is longed for like
nor**M**alcy in the midst of chaos
when **P**eace eludes, precludes the
inevitab**L**e onslaught of
irresolute **E**motions, naked
intentions e**X**posed –carry on

MECHANICAL

> Days on end
> I automatically move
> About doing what I always do
> Like the bottle capping machine
> I once saw at the Pepsi Cola Company
> Drop, cap, twist, raise, repeat...
> Bottle after mind numbing
> bottle moving past
> Days on end

NUMBER CRUNCHING
(a limerick)

My husband is quite analytical
And often a bit unpredictable.
"It's our twenty first year?
That's a century, my dear...
Soon it's one hundred months —hexadecimal."

I WOULD IF I COULD

I have never parasailed
Above the aqua water
Off Key West during sun set.
But I would if I could.

I have never played pat-a-cake
With a mischievous capuchin
Sitting in my lap.
But I would if I could.

I have never been to New York
To watch a hit musical
On Broadway.
But I would if I could.

I have never helicoptered
To Mendenhall Glacier
For a dog sled ride.
But I would if I could.

I have never gambled away
An entire year's salary
In Las Vegas.
But I could if I would.

LESSON IN HUMILITY
(a sestina)

Three weeks ago, when I was feeling vain
I scanned my fourth-grade class-that's when I spotted
something indicating a disease
dotting Jillian's cheeks and upturned nose.
I asked her if perchance the speckles itched;
and soon she was possessed by urgent scratching.

Our spelling champion, Jillian, would be scratching.
Her efforts for the bee had been in vain.
By Saturday her arms and legs were spotted;
"Bobby, my alternate, will go," she knows.
But Friday, Bobby's back and stomach itched.
His mother called, reporting his disease.

Chicken pox was clearly the disease
that had my stellar spellers ill and scratching.
Then Monday, at ten thirty on the nose,
while Sam read his report on weather vanes,
I noticed that his neck was sparsely spotted
and guessed his blotchy splotches surely itched.

I'd spurned the pox before, and now I itched
to vaccinate against the dread disease
before my fair complexion became spotted.
So, on my to-do list I started scratching,
"Call Doctor," hoping it was not in vain.
I can't be sick a week, God surely knows.

Now every savvy nurse and doctor knows
exposure to one student that has itched
means chicken pox will take its normal vein-
seize an entire classroom by disease.
Nothing stops the fever or the scratching.
Doc dismissed the notion I had spotted.

Tuesday, in the mirror a blotch was spotted
here, on my normally unblemished nose.
During penmanship I started scratching;
my nose wasn't the only thing that itched.
I finally had succumbed to the disease;
No longer was this teacher feeling vain.

Now, nearly well, I've tried in vain to make my skin less spotted.
This noxious, cruel disease has given me a beet red nose.
If you must know, I've itched in places itches defy scratching.

SOMETHING
THERE
IS
THAT
DOESN'T
LOVE
A
WALL

A nod to "Mending Wall" by Robert Frost

I often long to see beyond *something*
Such as the backyard fence that rises *there*.
Footfalls are heard but sight obstructed *is*,
So my mind forms a vivid image *that*,
Though false, deems fence deficient and *doesn't*
Calm, reassure, or boost neighborly *love*.
Thus, might seeing beyond spur in me *a*
Desire to take down existing *wall*?

(Golden Shovel poem)

HOW TO MEASURE   THE IMMEASUREABLE

Words can be measured in letters and sounds	Immeasurable is the weight of our words
By syllables, consonants, diphthongs and vowels	Some try to explore their mysterious worth
Through their inflection, their syntax and tone	But how they impact and why they endure
When spoken with other words or when alone	Is anyone's guess, not a soul can be sure
A touch can be light or heavy we know	Immeasurable is a touch's effect
As hard as a punch or as light as the snow	On indelible touches we often reflect
Whether in anger, in love or in grief	A touch can embarrass or cause one to weep
It's measured at times by how long or how brief	Then again, a mere brush may leave vestiges deep
Tears can be measured in grams or by drops	For causes of tears no measure exists
In passage of time before the tears stop	No depth of emotion, or length they persist
Comparison makes the measures replete	Tears flow from tenderness, sorrow, and pain
And sad equals salty while joy equals sweet	So crying when joyful is hard to explain
Into our lives come words, touches, and tears	No one can measure the love that God gives
God feels what we feel, he sees, and he hears	His love is defined in superlatives
His son was rejected, despised, betrayed	His love is the greatest, the strongest, the best
His measure of love is sin's debt that He paid	Its measure defies every trial and test

This poem is a Poetic Threesome.
The poem on the left and the poem on the right can each be read and understood independently.
When placed side by side and read across, the two poems form a separate third poem.

PLAY TIME

Done the duties of the day
Gone the others to their bed
How the words begin to play
Free at last inside my head

GUILTY

I've certainly stolen
Multiple chances
Great moves from dances
Hundreds of glances

I'm guilty of snatching
Kisses from babies
Petals from daisies
Spots that are shady

Oh, I have swiped
Cookie dough
Good jokes
Mementos

On many occasions I've
Taken a break
Taken a chance
Even taken the cake

I now confess to being a thief
Although my crimes
Have brought no grief
Still I will pay what is my due...

After taking a moment
To think this through.

POETIC INJUSTICE

A sonnet?
Doggone it!
Don't make me do it!
Not that I mind 'em
It's just that they
Kind of move in
So I'm
Dreaming and
Thinking,
Revising,
Improvising all in
Iambic pentameter
And I am no
Shakespeare
I am only an amateur
So anything else please,
Doggone it!
No sonnet!

WORD ART
(a limerick poem)

A wordsmith is what I profess
But here I must humbly confess
That the words that I write,
Be they noble and bright,
Rarely match what I hope to express.

Hundreds of eloquent words;
Nouns, prepositions and verbs
All neatly displayed
In a grammar-ly way
Yet I find them inane and absurd.

Compelling I fear they are not
But they're honestly all that I've got.
You say you've been blessed
By my creative mess?
I must be more ept than I thought!

WONDER

Causes my mind to dream

My heart to throb

My soul to dance.

DREAMS AND THINGS

Things are not what they seem;
All that is gold doesn't glitter.
But that's the thing—
It seldom matters,
Because all that glitters
Isn't gold either;
And a thing isn't beautiful
Because it lasts,
But because it grabs you
Refusing to let go
Like a thing possessed
Of nothing less than stardust
In your half-blind eyes.
Regardless,
A thing of beauty lasts forever
Unless it's a thing of the past;
And things of the past
Are memories made
Here or there or sometimes
In your meandering mind
That cuts and pastes
Bits and pieces
Calling it a masterpiece
When it is neither
Glitter nor gold
But moon dust.
And I could tell you
A thing or two about dreams
Made of moon dust.

I LOVE

I love light and air;
> music, poetry, birds, and cats;
> the laughter of children,
> the first signs of life in spring.

I love cinnamon rolls, chocolate, coffee,
> an occasional margarita or glass of wine;
> going barefoot to the garden;
> picking flowers and scrumptious fresh vegetables.

I love my house and the pond behind it;
> being lured by my husband for a romantic getaway in autumn;
> having long conversations about things that matter with my sons;
> doing girlie things-hair, shopping, nails- with my daughters-in-law.

I love extracting beauty from the ordinary: vegetables, fabric, flowers, weeds, words;
> sharing stories, songs, and hot chocolate with friends around a campfire;
> having little arms, not quite long enough to reach around me—try;
> guiding chubby little hands in forming their first letters.

I love the preparation for, anticipation of, and elation in performing music;
> long journeys by car across landscapes constantly changing;
> being in the midst of a crowd honoring the United States and her flag;
> offering loud and heartfelt praise to the one true God.

I love the quiet communion I enjoy with the Holy Spirit on long walks;
> heartwarming, gut-wrenching, and thought-provoking movies;
> being with people who make me laugh;
> the sense of pride and accomplishment that comes from working with my hands.

I love curling up on the sofa with a good book and at least one cat;
> the sweet scent of laundry dried on the clothesline;
> the simplicity and complexity of children's books;
> dressing up for special occasions.

I love snuggling into my jammies after a hard day of work;
> the fluid beauty of the sky;
> the pleasant surprise and peaceful repose of a snow day;
> the freedom I have in Christ to enjoy all of the things I love.

TEAL

my idea box
flea market owl
Grandmother's kitchen
blueberry flavored popsicles
the cove at Honeymoon Beach
sexy stilettos with pedicure to match
your eyes when you wear that sweater
paint for the guest room and bath
ribbons tied on golden pigtails
the chapel's vintage door
back of a bottle fly
our silk pillow
the sky in July

HOPE EMERGES

Throughout the barren winter and in the dark of night,
On dismal days when color is unexposed by light,
An altered life abides its self-made shell
While the things that best could lift it from out of the abyss
Expand, useless and crumpled inside the chrysalis.

Creature's plight could be perceived as pitiful mischance,
Restricted by its nature and blind by circumstance.
No future can prevail for one so dead.
Confounding recollections of a less than lustrous past
Transcend present existence by margin wide and vast.

Somehow, despite misgivings and elements endured
The creature feels a stirring, a tiny rip is heard.
Perhaps there is a future after all!
Then blinding rays invade the creature's dank and dreary space
Enlarging and exposing a life within that place.

Although its whole existence hangs by a silken thread
New warmth floods in, surrounds it, reviving what was dead.
"Alive for what?" the situation begs.
And now it finds the number of its legs has been reduced.
By whose sad misadventure was this tragedy induced?

It's now finished emerging from out its tight cocoon.
A tingling sensation spreads through its members soon.
Just what it means is more than one could guess.
Its wobbly legs are strengthened, and fresh air unfurls its wings,
Now swelling up with hope and fortitude that hoping brings.

For hours it sits immobile, yet quivers in the wind.
As transformation is complete, hues emerge and blend.
Life-sustaining blood now surges through.
Translucent, dazzling wings spread outward with uncanny ease,
And buoyed with hope the butterfly ascends upon a breeze.

THE REASON FOR A FLOWER

According to logic and scientific deduction
The reason for a flower is simply reproduction;
Stem, carpel, stamen, sepal, and petal
Amalgamated in purpose; united in function.

A bright floral cluster now illumines my vision.
I'm pressed for a deep philosophic decision.
Logic, emotion, heart-felt or factual?
My conclusion, by some, will be met with derision.

God chose to uniquely display His radiance
By brushing the landscape with swatches of elegance.
Sunflower, lily, hollyhock, laurel
Each subtly enhanced by splashes of fragrance.

When sorrow envelops, garlands sympathize.
When hope falters, rosebuds revitalize.
Posies declare me a friend, treasure, angel.
Where flowers abound, God is characterized.

Whether comfort, restoration, or love is most sought
A bouquet delivers, more often than not.
Visions of heaven, rare jewels, supernatural
Freely seen and accessible --inexpensively bought.

CLOTHESLINE CLEAN

She gives each pillowcase a snap;
Drapes the sheets across the line
And fastens them with wooden pins;
For wasting sunshine seems a sin
When summer breezes blow so fine,
Making bed sheets sway and flap.

From her kitchen now she sees
Linens curled; sheets unfurled
As if engaged in ritual,
Their antics light, ethereal
Waltzing garments whirl and twirl
Twixt greening grass and trees.

Soon bedding is collected,
Soft in arms outstretched
And hauled like treasure to the bed,
Sweet perfume filling her head
From bounteous load she's fetched
With scent of clean injected.

IMPOSSIBLE THINGS

Holding babies without kissing them
Leaving my love without missing him

Seeing a daffodil without smiling
Avoiding my kitten's eyes beguiling

Keeping my shoes on at the beach
Giving up dreams beyond my reach

MAMA'S GIFT

When life consisted of
Night feedings
Diapers and laundry
Mama would spend
A whole spring day
Washing my windows;
A strange choice of gifts
Perhaps.
But sparkling panes
Brought light and hope,
Enticed me to look beyond
The confining walls
Of motherhood,
Out at the birds
Clouds and sky.
Mama knew what
I know now-
Clean windows freshen
The weariest of spirits.
 dreams beyond my reach

OF HIM AND YOU
(a senryu poem)

Strange how love defies
Restriction, restraint, and time
needs no sustenance

He comments; you like
Touching as in the photo
Across time and space

Can so few keystrokes
Whittle away all the years
Stroke wondering hearts

INCONGRUITY

So many of life's necessities
Mowing
Cleaning
Laundering
Doing dishes
Straightening
Are not the things I live for
While the things I live for
Making music
Gardening
Travelling
Creating
Playing
Are hampered by life's necessities.

REVERIE

Walking no particular path
With no destination in mind
Meandering plodding panting
Unaware of exertion
My mind following
An alternate path sorting
The day's worries and cares
Until my feet stop
For no particular reason
Other than the feel
Of carpet beneath them
In this sepia toned wilderness

Moss as green as clover
Coats the rock on which I stand
And my breath
Catches in my chest
With the realization that
My mossy rock juts far
Far out from the bank
And its naked comrades
Disappearing into
This morning's mist
And now I can hear, not see
The river rushing
Far below and the deep
Emerald green draws
My blue eyes to the tree
Whose gnarled bare roots
Clutch the eroding bank

Up my eyes are drawn
Up beyond where the moss
Stopped climbing
Where only eagles wing
To reach their massive aerie
Atop the tree
Atop the rock
Atop the riverbank
Atop the world
That I Discovered
Quite by happenstance
Or Godly intervention

OF SKY AND SEA

age-old intriguing mystery
marriage of the sky and sea
from one man drinks the other breathes
two life-sustaining entities
on the horizon there they meet
ocean and firmament complete
a view of utmost majesty
stretched on unending tapestry
each reflecting what it sees
mirroring epitomes
cloud-cover, billow, ripple, breeze
azure, amber, ebony
taunting in versatility
yet fervent in stability
divided as our God decreed
merged as the open and the deep

SWITCH OFF THE LAMP

Let senses inhale the night

Muggy, with moonlight streaming in

Spring frog choirs chirping a cappella nearby

The faintest whisper of a breeze flutters across

Fresh-from-the-clothesline scented sheet pulled up

Hands reach, fingers lace, drawing the two of us together

Lips part, kiss lasts... lasts until breathing is necessary again

Muscles relax, thoughts abate; your breath soft on my cheek slows down

Hours or minutes pass

-which I do not know-

eyes flutter open

and dreamily I wonder

if moonlight, frog choirs,

sheets, breezes, and even you

lying by my side are dreamed or real;

for these are the very things that fairy tales are made of.

(a concrete poem)

JUST THE BASICS
(an ABC poem)

All I need is
Bible, books
Color
Daylight, dreams
Exercise
Faith
God
Hope and health
Inner peace
Joy
Kisses
Lemonade fresh made
Melodious music
Nighttime snuggles
Open doors
Positivity, peanut butter
Quiet times
Red roses- or pink
Summer and spring
Time to think
Windows and willows
X-tra sleep
Yesterdays
Zest for today

LASTS AND FIRSTS

The nearer the end becomes
The larger each last looms-
Lasts already past,
Like the never-ending apple harvest
I never dreamed would be the last;
Lasts that lie ahead,
Like locking doors and leaving keys behind
To things I love and leave with dread.

But beginnings will flourish
With firsts to fill each gap-
Long awaited firsts,
Like celebrations grand and small with tots
For whom this longing heart bursts;
Firsts that flabbergast,
Like blossoms found where none were thought to thrive-
Familiar ones with roots to past.

Made in the USA
Columbia, SC
21 March 2019